Manager Book, ESX7 (with exam answer sheet)	ISBN	978-1-58280-331-9
Manager Book, ESV7 (with online exam voucher)	ISBN	978-1-58280-330-2
Manager Book, ES7 (text only)	ISBN	978-1-58280-329-6

Printed in the USA
10 9 8 7 6 5 4 3 2 1

Contents

Staying Connected with the National Restaurant Association

The National Restaurant Association (NRA) has the resources and tools to support you throughout your education and career in the restaurant and foodservice industry. Through scholarships, educational programs, industry certifications, and member benefits, the NRA is your partner now and into the future.

Scholarships   The NRA's philanthropic foundation, the National Restaurant Association Educational Foundation (NRAEF), offers scholarships to college students through its NRAEF Scholarship Program. These scholarships can help pave your way to an affordable higher education and may be applied to a culinary, restaurant management, or foodservice-related program at an accredited college or university. We encourage you to investigate the opportunities, which include access to special program scholarships for ProStart students who earn the National Certificate of Achievement, as well as ManageFirst Program® students. You may be awarded one NRAEF scholarship per calendar year—make sure you keep applying every year! The NRAEF partners with state restaurant associations to offer student scholarships. Check with your state to see if they offer additional scholarship opportunities. The NRAEF also offers professional development scholarships for educators. Visit ChooseRestaurants.org/scholarships for information.

College education   As you research and apply to colleges and universities to continue your industry education, look for schools offering the NRA's ManageFirst Program. Just like Foundations of Restaurant Management & Culinary Arts, the ManageFirst Program and curriculum materials were developed with input from the restaurant and foodservice industry and academic partners. This management program teaches you practical skills needed to face real-world challenges in the industry, including interpersonal communication, ethics, accounting skills, and more. The program includes the ten topics listed below, plus ServSafe Food Safety and ServSafe Alcohol®:

- Controlling Foodservice Costs
- Hospitality and Restaurant Management
- Hospitality Human Resources Management and Supervision
- Customer Service
- Principles of Food and Beverage Management
- Purchasing
- Hospitality Accounting
- Bar and Beverage Management
- Nutrition
- Hospitality and Restaurant Marketing

Staying Connected with the National Restaurant Association

You can also earn the ManageFirst Professional® (MFP™) credential by passing five required ManageFirst exams and completing 800 work hours in the industry. Having the MFP on your resume tells employers that you have the management skills needed to succeed in the industry. To learn more about ManageFirst or to locate ManageFirst schools, visit managefirst. restaurant.org.

Certification In the competitive restaurant field, industry certifications can help you stand out among a crowd of applicants.

The NRA's ServSafe Food Protection Manager Certification is nationally recognized. Earning your certification tells the industry that you know food safety and the critical importance of its role—and enables you to share food safety knowledge with every other employee.

Through ServSafe Food Safety, you'll master sanitation, the flow of food through an operation, sanitary facilities, and pest management. ServSafe is the training that is learned, remembered, shared, and used. And that makes it the strongest food safety training choice for you. For more information on ServSafe, visit ServSafe.com.

The challenges surrounding alcohol service in restaurants have increased dramatically. To prepare you to address these challenges, the NRA offers ServSafe Alcohol. As you continue to work in the industry, responsible alcohol service is an issue that will touch your business, your customers, and your community. Armed with your ServSafe Alcohol Certificate, you can make an immediate impact on an establishment. Through the program, you'll learn essential responsible alcohol service information, including alcohol laws and responsibilities, evaluating intoxication levels, dealing with difficult situations, and checking identification. Please visit ServSafe.com/ alcohol to learn more about ServSafe Alcohol.

National Restaurant Association membership As you move into the industry, seek out careers in restaurants that are members of the NRA and your state restaurant association. Encourage any operation you are part of to join the national and state organizations. During your student years, the NRA also offers student memberships that give you access to industry research and information that can be an invaluable resource. For more information, or to join as a student member, visit restaurant.org.

Management credentials After you've established yourself in the industry, strive for the industry's highest management certification—the NRA's Foodservice Management Professional® (FMP®). The FMP certification recognizes exceptional managers and supervisors who have achieved the highest level of knowledge, experience, and professionalism that is most valued by our industry. You become eligible to apply and sit for the FMP exam after you've worked as a supervisor in the industry for three years. Passing the FMP exam places you in select company; you will have joined the ranks of leading industry professionals. The FMP certification is also an impressive credential to add to your title and resume. For more information on the Foodservice Management Professional certification, visit managefirst. restaurant.org.

Make the NRA your partner throughout your education and career. Take advantage of the NRA's scholarship, training, certification, and membership benefits that will launch you into your career of choice. Together we will lead this industry into an even brighter future.

Acknowledgments

The development of the *ServSafe Manager Book* would not have been possible without the expertise of our many advisors and manuscript reviewers. Thank you to the following people and organizations for their time, effort, and dedication to creating this seventh edition.

Chirag Bhatt, Bloomin' Brands, Inc.

Debra Boyette, Bojangles' Restaurants, Inc.

Linda Lockett Brown, CINET, Inc.

Kristie Costa, Rhode Island Hospitality Association

Joann DeTraglia, Mohawk Valley Community College

Jean Edsall, Compass Group

Matthew Jenkins, Sodexo

Chandra Johnson, Alpha Education

Kendra Kauppi, University of Minnesota

Mahmood Khan, Virginia Polytechnic Institute & State University

Shawn Kohlhaas, Culinary Cultivations

Jaymin Patel, Aramark

Kyle Reynolds, Le Cordon Bleu College of Culinary Arts

Jacob Rhoten, Cedar Fair Entertainment Co., Kings Dominion

Rachel Robinson, KFC/YUM Brands

Michael Sabella, Food Safety Certified, LLC

Gina Scammon, Suffolk County Department of Health New York

Jennifer Singman, Ecolab

Diane Withrow, Cape Fear Community College

Charles Yet, Washtenaw County Public Health

Providing Safe Food

Foodborne Illness at a Local Café

Dozens of people became sick at a small café. Guests who ate the café's famous baked potato salad called to complain of nausea and vomiting. These calls began within two days after eating the dish. Guests eventually experienced double vision and difficulty in speaking and swallowing.

The local regulatory authorities investigated. They found that the baked potatoes in the salad were the source of the outbreak. The potatoes had been wrapped in aluminum foil when they were baked. Then they were left on a prep table overnight to cool. Ultimately, the potatoes were left at room temperature for almost 18 hours before they were used in the salad. Bacteria on the potatoes had the correct conditions for growth.

You Can Prevent This

The guests became sick because the staff at the café did not know that baked potatoes might contain bacteria. When the staff did not handle the potatoes with care, bacteria on the potatoes grew to high levels. Preventing foodborne illnesses like this is one of your most important tasks as a manager. This chapter will introduce you to some basic concepts and principles for keeping food safe.

Study Questions

• What is a foodborne illness and what is a foodborne-illness outbreak?

• What are TCS and ready-to-eat food?

• What are the five risk factors for foodborne illness?

• Which populations have a higher risk for foodborne illness?

• How can you help to keep food safe in your operation?

• What are the roles of government agencies in keeping food safe?

Foodborne Illnesses

Being a foodservice manager is not easy. You have responsibilities to your operation, your staff, and your customers. The best way to meet those responsibilities is to keep the food you serve safe. To start, you must learn what foodborne illnesses are and the challenges you will face in preventing them. You simply can't afford not to. The costs of a foodborne-illness outbreak can be devastating.

Challenges to Food Safety

A foodborne illness is a disease transmitted to people by food. An illness is considered an outbreak when:

* Two or more people have the same symptoms after eating the same food.

* An investigation is conducted by state and local regulatory authorities.

* The outbreak is confirmed by a laboratory analysis.

Each year, millions of people get sick from unsafe food.

Foodservice operations work hard to minimize foodborne illnesses. As a result of these efforts, foodborne illnesses have declined in recent years. However, operations still face many challenges to food safety.

Time   Pressure to work quickly can make it hard to take the time to follow food safety practices.

Language and culture   Your staff may speak a different language than you do. This can make it difficult to communicate. Cultural differences can also influence how food handlers view food safety.

Literacy and education   Staff often have different levels of education. This makes it more challenging to teach them food safety.

Pathogens   Illness-causing microorganisms are more frequently found on types of food that once were considered safe.

Unapproved suppliers   Food that is received from suppliers that are not practicing food safety can cause a foodborne-illness outbreak.

High-risk customers   The number of customers at high risk for getting a foodborne illness is increasing. An example of this is the growing elderly population.

Staff turnover   Training new staff, as shown at left, leaves less time for food safety training.

The ServSafe program will provide you with the tools you need to overcome the challenges in managing a good food safety program.

The Cost of Foodborne Illnesses

Foodborne illnesses cost the United States billions of dollars each year. National Restaurant Association figures show that one foodborne-illness outbreak can cost an operation thousands of dollars. It can even result in closure. Some of these costs are shown in Table 1.1.

Table 1.1: **Costs of a Foodborne Illness to an Operation**

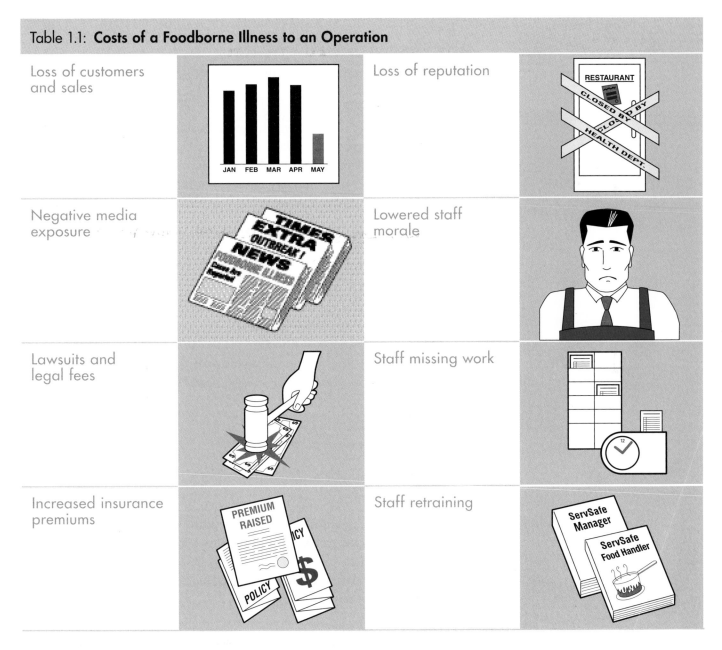

Loss of customers and sales	Loss of reputation
Negative media exposure	Lowered staff morale
Lawsuits and legal fees	Staff missing work
Increased insurance premiums	Staff retraining

Most important are the human costs. Victims of foodborne illnesses may experience the following:

- Lost work
- Medical costs
- Long-term disability
- Death

How Foodborne Illnesses Occur

Unsafe food is usually the result of contamination, which is the presence of harmful substances in food. To prevent foodborne illnesses, you must recognize the contaminants that can make food unsafe. These can come from pathogens, chemicals, or physical objects. They might also come from certain unsafe practices in your operation.

Contaminants

Contaminants are divided into three categories.

Biological   Pathogens are the greatest threat to food safety. They include certain viruses, parasites, fungi, and bacteria, as shown at left. Some plants, mushrooms, and seafood that carry harmful toxins (poisons) are also included in this group.

Bacteria— Time and Temperatures

Chemical   Foodservice chemicals can contaminate food if they are used incorrectly. The photo at left shows one example of how chemicals may contaminate food. Chemical contaminants can include cleaners, sanitizers, and polishes.

Physical   Foreign objects such as metal shavings, staples, and bandages can get into food. So can glass, dirt, and even bag ties. The photo at left shows this type of physical contaminant. Naturally occurring objects, such as fish bones in fillets, are another example.

Each of these contaminants is a danger to food safety. But biological contaminants are responsible for most foodborne illness.

How Food Becomes Unsafe

If food handlers do not handle food correctly, it can become unsafe. These are the five most common food-handling mistakes, or risk factors, that can cause a foodborne illness:

1 Purchasing food from unsafe sources

2 Failing to cook food correctly

3 Holding food at incorrect temperatures

4 Using contaminated equipment

5 Practicing poor personal hygiene

Purchasing food from unsafe sources can be a big problem. So, purchasing food from approved, reputable suppliers is critical. This will be discussed in greater detail later. Keep in mind that food prepared in a private home is also considered to be from an unsafe source and must be avoided. The other food handling mistakes listed are related to four main practices. These include time-temperature abuse, cross-contamination, poor personal hygiene, and poor cleaning and sanitizing. These are identified in Table 1.2 on the following page.

Something to Think About

More than 30 children experienced dizziness, nausea, and vomiting after eating spaghetti at an elementary school cafeteria. According to the regulatory authority, the spaghetti was not heated correctly on the day it was served. It also was not cooled correctly when it was prepared the day before. The cafeteria had to be closed so staff could be retrained on safe food-handling practices.

Table 1.2: **Practices Related to Foodborne Illness**

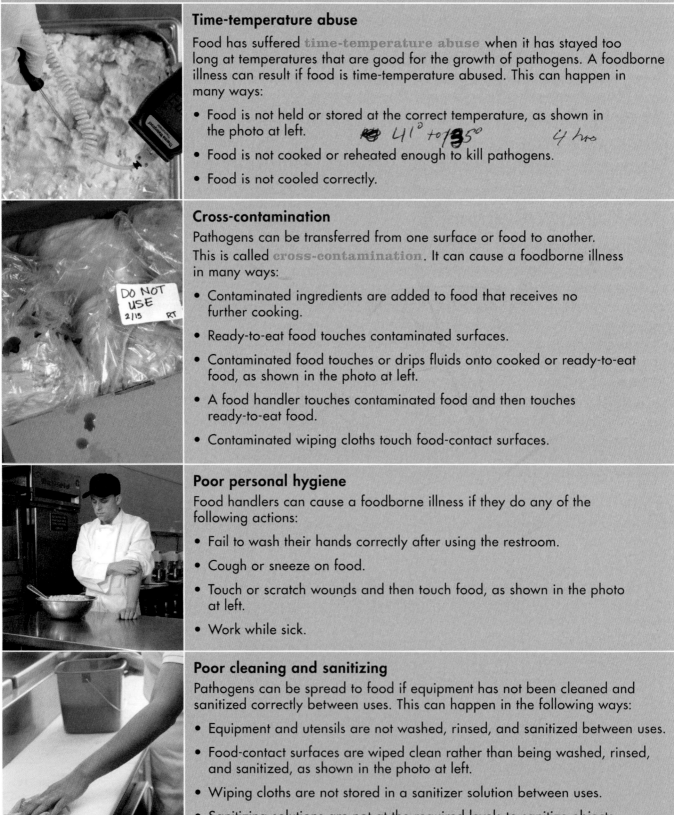

Time-temperature abuse

Food has suffered time-temperature abuse when it has stayed too long at temperatures that are good for the growth of pathogens. A foodborne illness can result if food is time-temperature abused. This can happen in many ways:

- Food is not held or stored at the correct temperature, as shown in the photo at left.
- Food is not cooked or reheated enough to kill pathogens.
- Food is not cooled correctly.

Cross-contamination

Pathogens can be transferred from one surface or food to another. This is called cross-contamination. It can cause a foodborne illness in many ways:

- Contaminated ingredients are added to food that receives no further cooking.
- Ready-to-eat food touches contaminated surfaces.
- Contaminated food touches or drips fluids onto cooked or ready-to-eat food, as shown in the photo at left.
- A food handler touches contaminated food and then touches ready-to-eat food.
- Contaminated wiping cloths touch food-contact surfaces.

Poor personal hygiene

Food handlers can cause a foodborne illness if they do any of the following actions:

- Fail to wash their hands correctly after using the restroom.
- Cough or sneeze on food.
- Touch or scratch wounds and then touch food, as shown in the photo at left.
- Work while sick.

Poor cleaning and sanitizing

Pathogens can be spread to food if equipment has not been cleaned and sanitized correctly between uses. This can happen in the following ways:

- Equipment and utensils are not washed, rinsed, and sanitized between uses.
- Food-contact surfaces are wiped clean rather than being washed, rinsed, and sanitized, as shown in the photo at left.
- Wiping cloths are not stored in a sanitizer solution between uses.
- Sanitizing solutions are not at the required levels to sanitize objects.

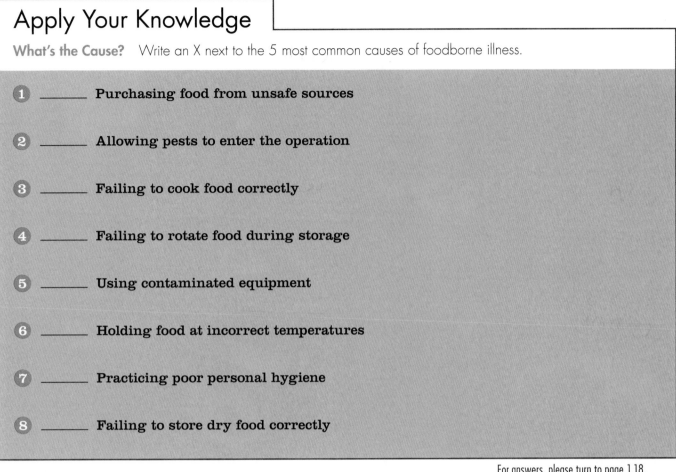

Apply Your Knowledge

What's the Cause?   Write an X next to the 5 most common causes of foodborne illness.

1 _____ **Purchasing food from unsafe sources**

2 _____ **Allowing pests to enter the operation**

3 _____ **Failing to cook food correctly**

4 _____ **Failing to rotate food during storage**

5 _____ **Using contaminated equipment**

6 _____ **Holding food at incorrect temperatures**

7 _____ **Practicing poor personal hygiene**

8 _____ **Failing to store dry food correctly**

For answers, please turn to page 1.18.

Food Most Likely to Become Unsafe

TCS and ready-to-eat food are the most likely types of food to become unsafe.

TCS Food

Pathogens grow well in TCS food. These items need time and temperature control to limit pathogen growth. For this reason, this food is called TCS food—food requiring time and temperature control for safety. TCS food is shown in Table 1.3 on the following page.

Table 1.3: TCS Food

	• Milk and dairy products	USDA	• Shell eggs (except those treated to eliminate nontyphoidal *Salmonella*)
USDA	• Meat: beef, pork, and lamb	USDA	• Poultry
USDA	• Fish		• Shellfish and crustaceans
	• Baked potatoes		• Heat-treated plant food, such as cooked rice, beans, and vegetables
	• Tofu or other soy protein • Synthetic ingredients, such as textured soy protein in meat alternatives		• Sprouts and sprout seeds Out
	• Sliced melons • Cut tomatoes • Cut leafy greens		• Untreated garlic-and-oil mixtures

Ready-to-Eat Food

Like TCS food, ready-to-eat food also needs careful handling
to prevent contamination. Ready-to-eat food is exactly what it
sounds like: food that can be eaten without further preparation,
washing, or cooking. Ready-to-eat food includes cooked food,
washed fruit and vegetables (whole and cut), and deli meat.
Bakery items and sugar, spices, and seasonings are
also included.

Populations at High Risk for Foodborne Illnesses

Certain groups of people have a higher risk of getting a
foodborne illness. These are listed in Table 1.4.

Table 1.4: High-Risk Populations

Elderly people
People's immune systems weaken with age. The
immune system is the body's defense against illness.

Preschool-age children
Very young children have not built up strong
immune systems.

People with compromised immune systems
Certain medical conditions and medications can
weaken a person's immune system. These include:

- Cancer or chemotherapy
- HIV/AIDS
- Transplants

Apply Your Knowledge

Which Is It?   Write an X next to the food that needs time and temperature control to keep it safe.

1 _____ **Chopped lettuce**

2 _____ **Sliced watermelon**

3 _____ **Dry rice**

4 _____ **Flour**

5 _____ **Cooked carrots**

6 _____ **Cheese**

Who Has a Greater Risk?   Write an X next to each group that has a higher risk of getting a foodborne illness because of their immune systems.

1 _____ **School teachers**

2 _____ **College students**

3 _____ **Preschool students**

4 _____ **Health-care providers**

5 _____ **Transplant recipients**

6 _____ **Nursing home residents**

For answers, please turn to page 1.18.

Keeping Food Safe

Now that you know how food can become unsafe, you can use this knowledge to keep food safe. Focus on these measures:

- Purchasing from approved, reputable suppliers
- Controlling time and temperature
- Preventing cross-contamination
- Practicing personal hygiene
- Cleaning and sanitizing

Set up standard operating procedures that focus on these areas. The ServSafe program will show you how to design these procedures in later chapters.

Training and Monitoring

As a manager, your job is more than just understanding food safety practices and creating the necessary procedures. You also must train your staff to follow these procedures, as shown in the photo at right. Staff should be trained when they are first hired and on an ongoing basis. Your entire staff needs general food safety knowledge. Other knowledge will be specific to the tasks performed on the job. For example, everyone needs to know the correct way to wash their hands. However, only receiving staff need to know how to inspect produce during receiving.

Staff need to be retrained in food safety regularly. When a food handler completes this training, document it.

Once staff are trained, monitor them to make sure they are following procedures. At times, you may notice employees doing tasks incorrectly. Each incorrect task could lead to an increase in risk. When this happens, it is important to correct the situation immediately. This is called corrective action. If an employee often completes a task incorrectly or if multiple employees complete a task incorrectly, they should be retrained.

Government Agencies Responsible for the Prevention of Foodborne Illness

Several government agencies take leading roles in the prevention of foodborne illness in the United States. The Food and Drug Administration (FDA) and the U.S. Department of Agriculture (USDA) inspect food and perform other critical duties.

Chicken   165°

State and local regulatory authorities create regulations and inspect operations, as shown in the photo at left.

Agencies such as the Centers for Disease Control and Prevention (CDC) and the U.S. Public Health Service (PHS) help with food safety as well.

The FDA

The FDA inspects all food except meat, poultry, and eggs. The agency also regulates food transported across state lines. In addition, the FDA issues a *Food Code*. This science-based code provides recommendations for food safety regulations. The *Food Code* was created for city, county, state, and tribal agencies. These agencies regulate foodservice for the following groups:

- Restaurants and retail food stores
- Vending operations
- Schools and day care centers
- Hospitals and nursing homes

Although the FDA recommends that states adopt the *Food Code*, it cannot require it. The FDA also provides technical support and training. This is available for industry and regulatory agencies.

Other Agencies

Several other agencies have an important role in food safety and the prevention of foodborne illness.

USDA   The U.S. Department of Agriculture regulates and inspects meat, poultry, and eggs. The USDA also regulates food that crosses state boundaries or involves more than one state.

CDC and PHS   These agencies assist the FDA, USDA, and state and local health departments. They conduct research into the causes of foodborne-illness outbreaks. They also assist in investigating outbreaks.

State and local regulatory authorities   Regulatory authorities write or adopt codes that regulate retail and foodservice operations. Codes may differ from the FDA *Food Code*, because these agencies are not required to adopt it.

Regulatory authorities have many responsibilities. Here are some of the responsibilities related to food safety:

- Inspecting operations
- Enforcing regulations
- Investigating complaints and illnesses
- Issuing licenses and permits
- Approving construction
- Reviewing and approving HACCP plans

Apply Your Knowledge

Who Does What?   Write the letter of the government agency in the space next to the action that agency takes. Some letters may be used more than once.

A. **FDA**

B. **USDA**

C. **CDC and PHS**

D. **State and local health departments**

① _FDA_ Writes the codes that regulate retail and foodservice operations

② _CDC_ Conducts research into the causes of foodborne-illness outbreaks

③ _USDA_ Inspects meat, poultry, and eggs

④ _____ Writes the *Food Code*

⑤ _State_ Inspects retail and foodservice operations

For answers, please turn to page 1.18.

Chapter Summary

- A foodborne illness is a disease transmitted to people by food. An illness is considered an outbreak when two or more people have the same symptoms after eating the same food.

- TCS and ready-to-eat food are especially at risk for contamination. TCS food is food that needs time and temperature control for safety. Ready-to-eat food is food that can be eaten without further preparation, washing, or cooking.

- There are five common risk factors that can cause a foodborne illness. These include (1) purchasing food from unsafe sources, (2) failing to cook food correctly, (3) holding food at incorrect temperatures, (4) using contaminated equipment, and (5) practicing poor personal hygiene. The risk factors are related to these unsafe practices: time-temperature abuse, cross-contamination, poor personal hygiene, and poor cleaning and sanitizing.

- Some groups are at a higher risk of getting sick from unsafe food. They include preschool-age children, elderly people, and people with compromised immune systems. Certain medical conditions and medications can compromise a person's immune system. These include cancer, chemotherapy, HIV/AIDS, and transplants.

- Important prevention measures for keeping food safe are controlling time and temperature; preventing cross-contamination; practicing good personal hygiene; purchasing from approved, reputable suppliers; and cleaning and sanitizing items correctly.

- Train your staff to follow safe food handling procedures. Train staff when they are hired and retrain them on an ongoing basis. Watch to make sure they follow procedures. If you see unsafe food handling practices, take corrective action to keep food safe. Retrain employees as needed.

- Federal, state, and local governments have a role in keeping food safe. The FDA issues the *Food Code*. The FDA, USDA, and state and local regulatory authorities regulate operations. These authorities issue operating permits and licenses for operations and have other responsibilities. The CDC and PHS conduct research and investigations related to food safety.

Chapter Review Case Study

Food safety is important to every foodservice operation, and the costs of a foodborne-illness outbreak can be high. However, you can avoid outbreaks by recognizing the importance of food safety, recognizing how food can become unsafe, identifying the risks associated with high-risk populations, training and monitoring staff, and following the keys to food safety.

Now, take what you have learned in this chapter and apply it to the following case study.

Lucas was not happy because he was working by himself. His coworker had called in sick, and they were expecting their regular Wednesday night group of softball players. Lucas was not feeling too well himself. On top of this, the large group canceled at the last minute. Unfortunately, Lucas had already started cooking a dozen burgers on the grill.

Lucas finished cooking the hamburger patties until they were well-done, and then he put them in a pan on the counter. "Maybe someone will order a burger later," he thought. Because there were no customers yet, he made a quick run to the restroom. When he finished, he wiped his hands on his apron, combed his hair, and headed back to the kitchen.

Twenty minutes later, Lucas got his first customers of the evening. They were an elderly man and his four-year-old granddaughter. Lucas was happy when they ordered a burger to share. "Cook it medium," the man said. It looked like the premade burgers would stay on the counter for a while.

Lucas went back to the kitchen and put a fresh patty on the grill. Then he wiped off the cutting board he had used earlier for prepping raw chicken. He sliced the tomatoes and onion. When the burger just passed medium-rare, he plated it up.

1 **What did Lucas do wrong?**

_____

_____

_____

2 **What should Lucas have done?**

_____

_____

_____

For answers, please turn to page 1.18.

Study Questions

Circle the best answer to each question.

1 **What is a foodborne-illness outbreak?**

A When two or more food handlers contaminate multiple food items

B When an operation serves contaminated food to two or more people

C When two or more people report the same illness from eating the same food

D When the CDC receives information on two or more people with the same illness

2 **Which is a ready-to-eat food?**

A Uncooked rice

B Raw deboned chicken

C Sea salt

D Unwashed green beans

3 **Why are preschool-age children at a higher risk for foodborne illnesses?**

A They have not built up strong immune systems.

B They are more likely to spend time in a hospital.

C They are more likely to suffer allergic reactions.

D Their appetites have increased since birth.

4 **Which is a TCS food?**

A Bread

B Flour

C Sprouts

D Strawberries

5 **The 5 common risk factors that can lead to foodborne illness are failing to cook food adequately, holding food at incorrect temperatures, using contaminated equipment, practicing poor personal hygiene, and**

A reheating leftover food.

B serving ready-to-eat food.

C using single-use, disposable gloves.

D purchasing food from unsafe sources.

Study Questions

6 Raw chicken breasts are left out at room temperature on a prep table. What is the risk that could cause a foodborne illness?

  A Cross-contamination

  B Poor personal hygiene

  C Time-temperature abuse

  D Poor cleaning and sanitizing

7 **What is TCS food?**

  A Food requiring thermometer checks for security

  B Food requiring trustworthy conditions for service

  C Food requiring training commitments for standards

  D Food requiring time and temperature control for safety

8 **A food handler left a pan of roasted turkey breasts to cool at room temperature overnight. In addition to throwing away the turkey, what is an appropriate corrective action?**

  A Complete an incident report.

  B Order additional turkey breasts.

  C Deduct the cost from the food handler's pay.

  D Make sure the food handler understands safe cooling practices.

9 **What is an important measure for preventing foodborne illness?**

  A Using new equipment

  B Measuring pathogens

  C Preventing cross-contamination

  D Serving locally grown, organic food

10 **What is one possible function of a government agency that is responsible for food safety?**

  A Ensuring a product's appeal

  B Approving a construction project

  C Monitoring an operation's revenue

  D Protecting a product's brand name

For answers, please turn to page 1.19.

Answers

1.7 What's the Cause?

1, 3, 5, 6, and 7 should be marked.

1.10 Which Is It?

1, 2, 5, and 6 should be marked.

1.10 Who Has a Greater Risk?

3, 5, and 6 should be marked.

1.13 Who Does What?

1 D

2 C

3 B

4 A

5 D

1.15 Chapter Review Case Study

Here is what Lucas did wrong:

- He came into work sick.

- He left cooked burgers sitting out at room temperature. This is time-temperature abuse.

- He wore his apron into the restroom. He also did not wash his hands after using the restroom and wiped his hands on his apron. This is poor personal hygiene.

- He sliced tomatoes on a cutting board that had been used for chicken. This is cross-contamination.

Answers

Here is what Lucas should have done:

- He should have called in sick. If Lucas was feeling sick, there is a chance he could have made his customers sick.

- When he realized he had made too many hamburger patties, he should have either stored the burgers in hot holding or thrown them out.

- He should have washed his hands after using the bathroom and after touching his hair. He should have removed his apron before using the restroom.

- When slicing the tomatoes, Lucas should have first washed, rinsed, and sanitized the cutting board. Also, he could have used a separate cutting board.

1.16 Study Questions

1 C
2 C
3 A
4 C
5 D
6 C
7 D
8 D
9 C
10 B

2

Forms of
Contamination

Shigella Outbreak

Sixteen guests and three catering hall staff became sick with *Shigella* spp. They ate at a popular catering hall located in the southeastern United States.

Within one to three days after the catered event, reports began to come in to the local regulatory authority. Those who had gotten sick reported very similar symptoms. Each had experienced stomach cramps, fever, and diarrhea. Three people went to the emergency room to seek treatment.

The specific food involved was never determined. But the regulatory authority confirmed that the outbreak was likely caused by the catering hall's lead cook, who had prepped the food served at the luncheon. He was not feeling well the morning of the luncheon when he reported to work. He also had failed to wash his hands many times during his morning shift.

The catering hall's management team worked with the local regulatory authority to change procedures for dealing with staff illnesses. They also started an aggressive training program that focused on correct handwashing.

You Can Prevent This

Illnesses such as the one in the story above can be prevented if you understand how pathogens contaminate food. It is also important to prevent other items, such as chemicals and physical objects, from contaminating food.

Study Questions

- What are biological, chemical, and physical contaminants and how can you prevent food from being contaminated by them?

- How can the deliberate contamination of food be prevented?

- What is the correct response to a foodborne-illness outbreak?

- What are the most common food allergens and how can you prevent exposure to food allergens?

Biological, Chemical, and Physical Contaminants

One of the foodservice manager's most important roles is to prevent any type of contamination of food from occurring. Contamination is the presence of harmful substances in food. Those substances can be biological, chemical, or physical. Most contaminants cause foodborne illness. Others can result in physical injury.

How Contamination Happens

Contaminants come from a variety of places. Many contaminants are found in the animals we use for food. Others come from the air, contaminated water, and dirt. Some contaminants come from the chemicals we use in our operations. Others occur naturally in food, such as the bones in fish.

Food can be contaminated on purpose. But most food contamination happens accidentally. Most contaminants get into food and onto food-contact surfaces because of the way that people handle them. For example, food handlers who do not wash their hands after using the restroom may contaminate food and surfaces with feces from their fingers. Once the food that the food handler touched is eaten, a foodborne illness may result. This is called the fecal-oral route of contamination.

Food handlers can also pass on contaminants when they are in contact with a person who is sick. Some contaminants are passed very easily in any of these ways:

- From person to person

- Through sneezing or vomiting onto food or food-contact surfaces

- From touching dirty food-contact surfaces and equipment, and then touching food

Simple mistakes can result in contamination. For example, ready-to-eat food can become contaminated if it touches a surface that had contact with raw meat, seafood, and poultry. An example is shown in the photo at left. Storing food incorrectly or cleaning produce incorrectly can also lead to contamination. So can the failure to spot signs of pests in the operation, because pests are a major source of disease.

Biological Contamination

Biological contamination occurs from microorganisms. These are small, living organisms that can be seen only through a microscope. Many microorganisms are harmless, but some can cause illness. Harmful microorganisms are called pathogens. Some pathogens make you sick when you eat them. Others produce poisons—or toxins—that make you sick.

Understanding these biological contaminants is the first step to preventing foodborne-illness outbreaks. There are four types of pathogens that can contaminate food and cause foodborne illness. These are bacteria, viruses, parasites, and fungi (which includes molds and yeast).

According to the Food and Drug Administration (FDA), there are over 40 kinds of bacteria, viruses, parasites, and molds that can occur in food and cause a foodborne illness. Of these, six have been singled out by the FDA. These have been dubbed the Big Six because they are highly contagious and can cause severe illness. The Big Six include the following:

- *Shigella* spp.
- *Salmonella* Typhi
- Nontyphoidal *Salmonella* (NTS)
- Shiga toxin-producing *Escherichia coli* (STEC), also known as *E. coli*
- Hepatitis A
- Norovirus

Symptoms of Foodborne Illness

The symptoms of a foodborne illness vary, depending on which illness a person has. But most victims of foodborne illness share some common symptoms:

- Diarrhea
- Vomiting
- Fever
- Nausea
- Abdominal cramps
- Jaundice (a yellowing of the skin and eyes), shown at right

Not every person who is sick with a foodborne illness will have all of these symptoms. Nor are the symptoms of a foodborne illness limited to this list.

How quickly foodborne-illness symptoms appear in a person is known as the onset time of the illness. Onset times depend on the type of foodborne illness a person has. They can range from 30 minutes to as long as six weeks. How severe the illness is can also vary, from mild diarrhea to death.

Bacteria

Bacteria that cause foodborne illness have some basic characteristics.

Location   Bacteria can be found almost everywhere. They live in and on our bodies. Some types of bacteria keep us healthy, while others cause illness.

Detection   Bacteria cannot be seen, smelled, or tasted.

Growth   Bacteria need six conditions to grow. You can remember these conditions by thinking of the words FAT TOM, explained in Table 2.1. If FAT TOM conditions are correct, bacteria will grow in rapid numbers.

Prevention   The most important way to prevent bacteria from causing a foodborne illness is to control time and temperature.

Table 2.1: **FAT TOM—Conditions for Bacteria to Grow**

Food
Most bacteria need nutrients to survive. TCS food supports the growth of bacteria better than other types of food.

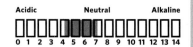

Acidic   Neutral   Alkaline
0 1 2 3 4 5 6 7 8 9 10 11 12 13 14

Acidity
Bacteria grow best in food that contains little or no acid. pH is the measure of acidity. The pH scale ranges from 0 to 14.0. A value of 0 is highly acidic, while a value of 14 is highly alkaline. A pH of 7 is neutral. Bacteria grows best in food that is neutral to slightly acidic.

Temperature
Bacteria grow rapidly between 41°F and 135°F (5°C and 57°C). This range is known as the temperature danger zone. Bacteria grow even more rapidly from 70°F to 125°F (21°C to 52°C). Bacteria growth is limited when food is held above or below the temperature danger zone.

Table 2.1: FAT TOM—Conditions for Bacteria to Grow *(continued)*

	Time Bacteria need time to grow. The more time bacteria spend in the temperature danger zone, the more opportunity they have to grow to unsafe levels.
	Oxygen Some bacteria need oxygen to grow. Others grow when oxygen is not there.
	Moisture Bacteria grow well in food with high levels of moisture. The amount of moisture available in food for this growth is called water activity (a_w). The a_w scale ranges from 0.0 to 1.0. The higher the value, the more available moisture in the food. For example, water has a water activity of 1.0.

Controlling FAT TOM Conditions

You can help keep food safe by controlling FAT TOM. In your operation, however, you will most likely be able to control only time and temperature.

- To control temperature, you must do your best to keep TCS food out of the temperature danger zone.

- To control time, you must limit how long food spends in the temperature danger zone.

Major Bacteria That Cause Foodborne Illness

Many types of bacteria can cause a foodborne illness. The FDA has identified four in particular that are highly contagious and can cause severe illness:

- *Salmonella* Typhi

- Nontyphoidal *Salmonella* (**NTS**)

- *Shigella* spp.

- Shiga toxin-producing *E. coli* (**STEC**)

These bacteria are described in Table 2.2 on the following page. Food handlers diagnosed with illnesses from these bacteria must **NEVER** work in a foodservice operation while they are sick.

Table 2.2: Major Bacteria That Cause Foodborne Illness

Bacteria	Source	Food Linked with the Bacteria	Prevention Measures
Salmonella Typhi (SAL-me-NEL-uh TI-fee)	*Salmonella* Typhi lives only in humans. People with typhoid fever carry the bacteria in their bloodstream and intestinal tract. Eating only a small amount of these bacteria can make a person sick. The severity of symptoms depends on the health of the person and the amount of bacteria eaten. The bacteria are often in a person's feces for weeks after symptoms have ended.	• Ready-to-eat food • Beverages	• Exclude from the operation food handlers who have been diagnosed with an illness caused by *Salmonella* Typhi. • Wash hands. • Cook food to minimum internal temperatures.
Nontyphoidal *Salmonella* (NON-ti-FOY-dal SAL-me-NEL-uh)	Many farm animals carry nontyphoidal *Salmonella* naturally. Eating only a small amount of these bacteria can make a person sick. How severe symptoms are depends on the health of the person and the amount of bacteria eaten. The bacteria are often in a person's feces for weeks after symptoms have ended.	• Poultry and eggs • Meat • Milk and dairy products • Produce, such as tomatoes, peppers, and cantaloupes	• Cook poultry and eggs to minimum internal temperatures. • Prevent cross-contamination between poultry and ready-to-eat food. • Exclude from the operation food handlers who are vomiting or have diarrhea and have been diagnosed with an illness caused by nontyphoidal *Salmonella*.

Table 2.2: **Major Bacteria That Cause Foodborne Illness** (continued)

Bacteria	Source	Food Linked with the Bacteria	Prevention Measures
Shigella spp. (shi-GEL-uh)	*Shigella* spp. is found in the feces of humans with the illness. Most illnesses occur when people eat or drink contaminated food or water. Flies can also transfer the bacteria from feces to food. Eating only a small amount of these bacteria can make a person sick. High levels of the bacteria are often in a person's feces for weeks after symptoms have ended.	• Food that is easily contaminated by hands, such as salads containing TCS food (potato, tuna, shrimp, macaroni, and chicken) • Food that has made contact with contaminated water, such as produce	• Exclude from the operation food handlers who have diarrhea and have been diagnosed with an illness caused by *Shigella* spp. • Wash hands. • Control flies inside and outside the operation.
Shiga toxin-producing *Escherichia coli* (ess-chur-EE-kee-UH KO-LI) (STEC), also known as *E. coli*	Shiga toxin-producing *E. coli* can be found in the intestines of cattle. The bacteria can contaminate meat during slaughtering. The bacteria is also found in infected people. Eating only a small amount of the bacteria can make a person sick. Once eaten, it produces toxins in the intestines, which cause the illness. The bacteria are often in a person's feces for weeks after symptoms have ended.	• Ground beef (raw and undercooked) • Contaminated produce	• Exclude from the operation food handlers who have diarrhea and have been diagnosed with a disease from the bacteria. • Cook food, especially ground beef, to minimum internal temperatures. • Purchase produce from approved, reputable suppliers. • Prevent cross-contamination between raw meat and ready-to-eat food.

Viruses

Viruses share some basic characteristics.

Location   Viruses are carried by human beings and animals. They require a living host to grow. While viruses do not grow in food, they can be transferred through food and still remain infectious in food.

Sources   People can get viruses from food, water, or any contaminated surface. Foodborne illnesses from viruses typically occur through fecal-oral routes. Norovirus is one of the leading causes of foodborne illness. It is often transmitted through airborne vomit particles.

Destruction   Viruses are not destroyed by normal cooking temperatures. That is why it is especially important to practice good personal hygiene when handling food and food-contact surfaces. The quick removal and cleanup of vomit is also important.

Major Viruses That Cause Foodborne Illness

The FDA has identified two viruses in particular that are highly contagious and can cause severe illness:

- Hepatitis A
- Norovirus

These viruses are described in Table 2.3. Food handlers diagnosed with Hepatitis A or Norovirus must **NOT** work in a foodservice operation while they are sick.

Table 2.3: Major Viruses That Cause Foodborne Illness

Virus	Source	Food Linked with the Virus	Prevention Measures
Hepatitis A	Hepatitis A is mainly found in the feces of people infected with it. The virus can contaminate water and many types of food. It is commonly linked with ready-to-eat food. However, it has also been linked with shellfish from contaminated water. The virus is often transferred to food when infected food handlers touch food or equipment with fingers that have feces on them. Eating only a small amount of the virus can make a person sick. An infected person may not show symptoms for weeks but can be very infectious. Cooking does not destroy Hepatitis A.	• Ready-to-eat food • Shellfish from contaminated water	• Exclude from the operation food handlers who have been diagnosed with Hepatitis A. • Exclude from the operation food handlers who have had jaundice for seven days or less. • Wash hands. • Avoid bare-hand contact with ready-to-eat food. • Purchase shellfish from approved, reputable suppliers.
Norovirus	Like Hepatitis A, Norovirus is commonly linked with ready-to-eat food. It has also been linked with contaminated water. Norovirus is often transferred to food when infected food handlers touch food or equipment with fingers that are contaminated by feces. Eating only a small amount of Norovirus can make a person sick. It is also very contagious. People become contagious within a few hours after eating it. The virus is often in a person's feces for days after symptoms have ended.	• Ready-to-eat food • Shellfish from contaminated water	• Exclude from the operation food handlers who are vomiting or have diarrhea and have been diagnosed with Norovirus. • Wash hands. • Avoid bare-hand contact with ready-to-eat food. • Purchase shellfish from approved, reputable suppliers.

Parasites

Parasites share some basic characteristics.

Location   Parasites require a host to live and reproduce.

Sources   Parasites are commonly associated with seafood, wild game, and food processed with contaminated water, such as produce.

Prevention   The most important way to prevent foodborne illnesses from parasites is to purchase food from approved, reputable suppliers. Cooking food to required minimum internal temperatures is also important. Make sure that fish that will be served raw or undercooked has been correctly frozen by the manufacturer.

Fungi

Fungi include yeasts, molds, and mushrooms. Some molds and mushrooms produce toxins that cause foodborne illness. Throw out all moldy food unless the mold is a natural part of the food. Because harmful mushrooms are difficult to recognize, you must purchase all mushrooms from approved, reputable suppliers.

Biological Toxins

Most foodborne illnesses are caused by pathogens—a form of biological contamination. But you also must be aware of biological toxins or poisons that can make people sick.

Origin   Some toxins are naturally associated with certain plants, mushrooms, and seafood. Toxins are a natural part of some fish. Other toxins, such as histamine, are made by pathogens on the fish when it is time-temperature abused. This can occur in tuna, bonito, mackerel, and mahimahi. Some fish become contaminated when they eat smaller fish that have eaten a toxin. One of these toxins is the ciguatera toxin. It can be found in barracuda, snapper, grouper, and amberjack. Shellfish, such as oysters, can be contaminated when they eat marine algae that have a toxin.

Symptoms   Many types of illnesses can occur from eating seafood toxins. Each of these has specific symptoms and onset times. In general, however, people will experience an illness within minutes of eating the toxin. Depending upon the illness, symptoms can include diarrhea or vomiting. Neurological symptoms may also appear, such as tingling in the extremities and the reversal of hot and cold sensations. People may also experience flushing of the face, difficulty breathing, burning in the mouth, heart palpitations, and hives.

Prevention   Toxins cannot be destroyed by cooking or freezing. The most important way to prevent a foodborne illness is to purchase plants, mushrooms, and seafood from approved, reputable suppliers. It is also important to control time and temperature when handling raw fish.

Other Pathogens

The pathogens discussed throughout this chapter are not the only ones that can cause a foodborne illness. See the appendix for a comprehensive list of pathogens that can affect food safety.

Chemical Contaminants

Many people have gotten sick after consuming food and beverages contaminated with foodservice chemicals. To keep food safe, follow these guidelines.

Sources   Chemicals can contaminate food if they are used or stored incorrectly. Cleaners, sanitizers, polishes, machine lubricants, and pesticides can be risks. Also included are deodorizers, first-aid products, and health and beauty products, such as hand lotions and hairsprays. The food handler in the photo at right is spraying chemicals too close to the food.

Certain types of kitchenware and equipment also can be risks for chemical contamination. These include items made from pewter, copper, zinc, and some types of painted pottery. These materials are not always safe for food and can cause contamination. This is especially true when acidic food, such as tomato sauce, is held in them, as seen in the photo at right.

Symptoms   Symptoms vary depending on the chemical consumed. Most illnesses occur within minutes. Vomiting and diarrhea are typical. If an illness is suspected, call the emergency number in your area and the Poison Control number.

Prevention   The chemicals you use must be approved for use in a foodservice operation. They must also be necessary for the maintenance of the facility. Here are some ways to protect food and food-contact surfaces from contamination by chemicals:

- Purchase chemicals from approved, reputable suppliers.

- Store chemicals away from prep areas, food-storage areas, and service areas. Chemicals must be separated from food and food-contact surfaces by spacing and partitioning, as seen in the photo at right. Chemicals must **NEVER** be stored above food or food-contact surfaces.

- Use chemicals for their intended use and follow the manufacturer's directions.

- Only handle food with equipment and utensils approved for foodservice use.

- Make sure the manufacturer's labels on original chemical containers are readable.

- Follow the manufacturer's directions and local regulatory requirements when throwing out chemicals.

Physical Contaminants

Food can become contaminated when objects get into it. It can also happen when natural objects are left in food, like bones in a fish fillet.

Sources   Some common objects that can get into food include metal shavings from cans, wood, fingernails, staples, bandages, glass, jewelry, and dirt. Naturally occurring objects, such as fruit pits and bones, can also be contaminants.

Symptoms   Mild to fatal injuries are possible. This could include cuts, dental damage, and choking. Bleeding and pain may be the most outward symptoms.

Prevention   Purchase food from approved, reputable suppliers to prevent physical contamination. Closely inspect the food you receive. Take steps to make sure no physical contaminants can get into it. This includes making sure that food handlers practice good personal hygiene.

Apply Your Knowledge

Which Ones Are Contaminants?   Write an X next to each item that can be a physical contaminant.

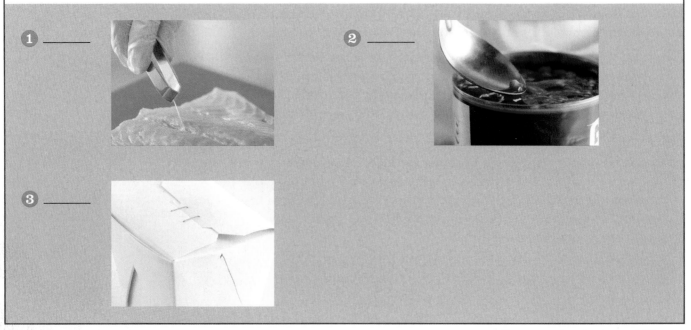

1 _____

2 _____

3 _____

For answers, please turn to page 2.32.

Apply Your Knowledge

What's Wrong with This Picture?   Write an X next to each picture that shows an unsafe practice when handling chemicals.

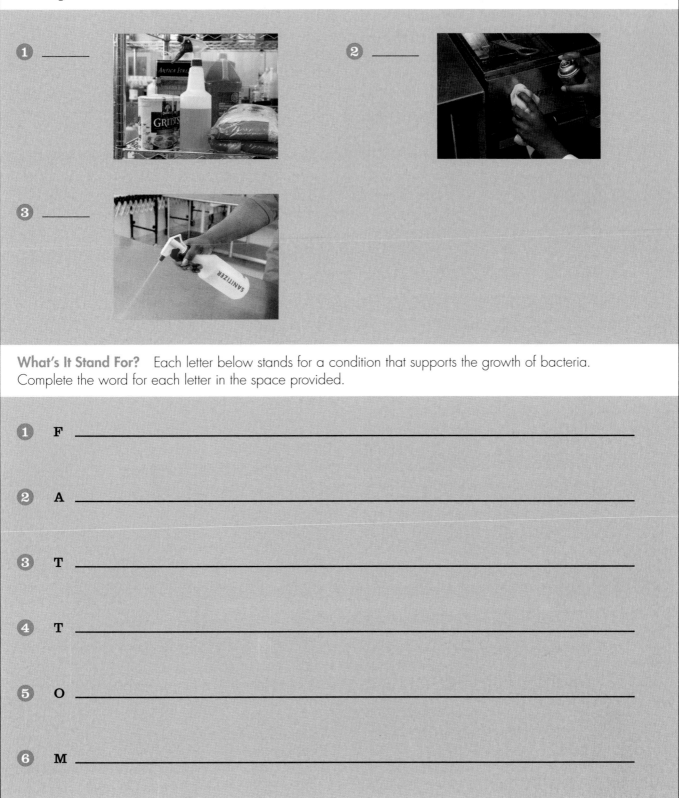

1 _____

2 _____

3 _____

What's It Stand For?   Each letter below stands for a condition that supports the growth of bacteria. Complete the word for each letter in the space provided.

1 **F** _____

2 **A** _____

3 **T** _____

4 **T** _____

5 **O** _____

6 **M** _____

For answers, please turn to page 2.32.

Apply Your Knowledge

Who Am I?   Identify the pathogen from the description given and write its name in the space provided.

1 • I am commonly linked with ready-to-eat food.

   • I am found in the feces of infected people.

   • Excluding staff with jaundice can stop me.

   • Handwashing can prevent me.

_____

_____

_____

_____

2 • I am carried in the bloodstream and intestinal tract of humans.

   • I am commonly linked with beverages and ready-to-eat food.

   • Cooking food correctly can prevent me.

   • Washing hands can stop me.

_____

_____

_____

_____

3 • Many farm animals carry me naturally.

   • I have been found in milk and dairy products, produce, and poultry.

   • Cooking eggs to minimum internal temperatures can prevent me.

   • Preventing cross-contamination between poultry and ready-to-eat food can stop me.

_____

_____

_____

_____

For answers, please turn to page 2.32.

Apply Your Knowledge

What's the Best Way to Control Them?   Write the letter of the most important prevention measure for each pathogen in the space provided. Some letters may be used more than once.

A Control time and temperature

B Practice correct personal hygiene

C Purchase from approved, reputable suppliers

1 __A__ Bacteria
2 __B__ Viruses
3 _____ Parasites
4 _____ Fungi

5 _____ Plant toxins
6 _____ Mushroom toxins
7 __A__ Seafood toxins

For answers, please turn to page 2.33.

Deliberate Contamination of Food

So far, you have learned about methods to prevent the accidental contamination of food. But you also must take steps to stop people who are actually trying to contaminate it. This may include the following groups:

- Terrorists or activists
- Disgruntled current or former staff
- Vendors
- Competitors

These people may try to tamper with your food using biological, chemical, or physical contaminants. They may even use radioactive materials. Attacks might occur anywhere in the food supply chain. But they are usually focused on a specific food item, process, or business.

The best way to protect food is to make it as difficult as possible for someone to tamper with it. For this reason, a food defense program should deal with the points in your operation where food is at risk. The FDA has created a tool that can be used to develop a food defense program. It is based on the acronym A.L.E.R.T. It can be used to help you identify the points in your operation where food is at risk.

Assure   Make sure that products you receive are from safe sources:

- Supervise product deliveries.
- Use approved suppliers who practice food defense.
- Request that delivery vehicles are locked or sealed.

Look   Monitor the security of products in the facility:

- Limit access to prep and storage areas. Locking storage areas is one way to do this, as shown in the photo at left.
- Create a system for handling damaged products.
- Store chemicals in a secure location.
- Train staff to spot food defense threats.

Employees   Know who is in your facility:

- Limit access to prep and storage areas.
- Identify all visitors, and verify credentials.
- Conduct background checks on staff.

Reports   Keep information related to food defense accessible:

- Receiving logs
- Office files and documents
- Staff files
- Random food defense self-inspections

Threat   Identify what you will do and who you will contact if there is suspicious activity or a threat at your operation:

- Hold any product you suspect to be contaminated.
- Contact your regulatory authority immediately.
- Maintain an emergency contact list.

Something to Think About

In the fall of 1984, the single largest bioterrorist attack in the United States occurred. It was carried out by members of a cult who had hoped to influence the turnout of a local election. They sprinkled a liquid containing *Salmonella* Typhimurium on salad bars at 10 local restaurants. As a result, over 750 people got sick, with 45 being hospitalized. Fortunately, there were no fatalities.

Apply Your Knowledge

The Best Defense   Write an X next to the practices that may be a risk to food defense.

1 _____ Limiting access to prep areas

2 _____ Giving staff access to all storage areas

3 _____ Storing chemicals in a locked storage area

4 _____ Buying produce from the local farmer's market

5 _____ Giving tours of the kitchen to the general public

6 _____ Holding products that you suspect are contaminated

7 _____ Allowing delivery drivers to store products in coolers

8 _____ Accepting food deliveries from trucks that have not been kept locked

For answers, please turn to page 2.33.

Responding to a Foodborne-Illness Outbreak

Despite your best efforts, a foodborne-illness outbreak may occur. Here are some things you should consider when responding to an outbreak.

Gathering information   Ask the person making the complaint for general contact information and to identify the food that was eaten. Also ask for a description of symptoms and when the person first became sick.

Notifying authorities   Contact the local regulatory authority if you suspect an outbreak.

Segregating product   Set the suspected product aside if any remains. Include a label with "Do Not Use" and "Do Not Discard" on it, as shown in the photo at left.

Documenting information   Log information about the suspected product. This might include a product description, production date, and lot number. The sell-by date and pack size should also be recorded.

Identifying staff   Maintain a list of food handlers scheduled at the time of the suspected contamination. These staff members may be subject to an interview and sampling by investigators. They should also be interviewed immediately by management about their health status.

Cooperating with authorities   Cooperate with regulatory authorities in the investigation. Provide appropriate documentation. You may be asked to provide temperature logs, HACCP documents, staff files, etc.

Reviewing procedures   Review food handling procedures to identify if standards are not being met or procedures are not working.

Apply Your Knowledge

Handling a Foodborne-Illness Outbreak   Read the story below and determine whether the situation was handled correctly. Then identify what Emma did right and what she did wrong.

Emma, the manager of Tiny's Sandwich Shop, took a phone call from a customer who complained of diarrhea and vomiting after eating a tuna salad sandwich the day before. Emma was not worried about the complaint, but she interviewed the customer for details anyway. After several more calls like that one, she knew there was a problem. Emma threw away all of the tuna salad so no one else would get sick. Then she called her local regulatory authority for guidance. While she was waiting for the authority to arrive, she made a list of the staff who were working the day before.

1 What did Emma do right?

_____

_____

_____

_____

2 What did Emma do wrong?

_____

_____

_____

_____

For answers, please turn to page 2.33.

Food Allergens

A food allergen is a protein in a food or ingredient that some people are sensitive to. These proteins occur naturally. When enough of an allergen is eaten, an allergic reaction can occur. This is when the immune system mistakenly considers the allergen to be harmful and attacks the food protein. There are specific signs that a customer is having an allergic reaction. To protect your customers, you should be able to recognize these signs and know what to do. You also should know the types of food that most often cause allergic reactions to help prevent them from happening.

Allergy Symptoms

Depending on the person, an allergic reaction can happen just after the food is eaten or several hours later. This reaction could include some or all of these symptoms:

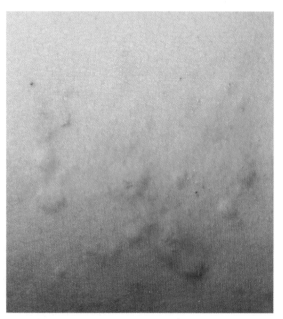

- Nausea
- Wheezing or shortness of breath
- Hives or itchy rashes, as shown in the photo at left
- Swelling of various parts of the body, including the face, eyes, hands, or feet
- Vomiting and/or diarrhea
- Abdominal pain
- Itchy throat

Initially symptoms may be mild, but they can become serious quickly. In severe cases, anaphylaxis—a severe allergic reaction that can lead to death—may result. If a customer is having a severe allergic reaction to food, call the emergency number in your area and inform them of the allergic reaction.

Common Food Allergens

You and your staff must be aware of the most common food allergens and the menu items that contain them.

While more than 160 food items can cause allergic reactions, just eight of those account for 90 percent of all reactions in the United States. These eight food items are known as the Big Eight and are shown in Table 2.4.

Table 2.4: **The Big Eight Allergens**

Milk		Soy	
Eggs		Wheat	
Fish, such as bass, flounder, and cod		Crustacean shellfish, such as crab, lobster, and shrimp	
Peanuts		Tree nuts, such as walnuts and pecans	

Preventing Allergic Reactions

Fifteen million Americans have a food allergy, and allergic reactions result in 200,000 emergency room visits every year. Both service staff and kitchen staff need to do their part to avoid serving food containing allergens to people with food allergies. These precautions also apply to any food sensitivities that a customer might mention, such as a gluten intolerance.

Calories per gram:
Fat 9 • Carbohydrate 4 • Protein 4

INGREDIENTS: CHICKEN BROTH, CONTAINS LESS THAN 1% OF THE FOLLOWING: SALT, DEXTROSE, CHICKEN FAT, MONOSODIUM GLUTAMATE, HYDROLYZED WHEAT GLUTEN, NATURAL FLAVORS, AUTOLYZED YEAST EXTRACT, CARROT JUICE CONCENTRATE, MONO AND DIGLYCERIDES, XANTHAN GUM, ONION JUICE CONCENTRATE.

CONTAINS: WHEAT.

Food Labels

Food labels are an important tool used to identify allergens in the products that you purchase. Federal law requires manufactured products containing one or more of the Big Eight allergens to clearly identify them on the ingredient label. The allergen may be included in the common name of the food, such as buttermilk, or it may be shown in parentheses after the ingredient. Often, allergens will be shown in a "contains" statement, such as in the photo at left.

Service Staff

Your staff should be able to tell customers about menu items that contain potential allergens. At minimum, have one person available per shift to answer customers' questions about menu items. When customers say they have a food allergy, your staff should take it seriously. When working with a customer to place an allergen special order, they must be able to do the following.

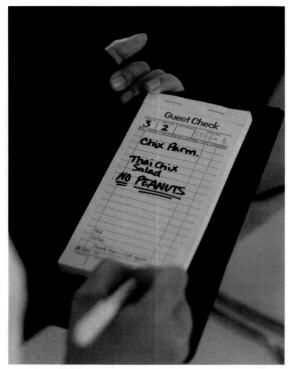

Describe dishes   Tell customers how the item is prepared. Sauces, marinades, and garnishes often contain allergens. For example, peanut butter is sometimes used as a thickener in sauces or marinades. This information is critical to a customer with a peanut allergy.

Identify ingredients   Tell customers if the food they are allergic to is in the menu item. Identify any "secret" ingredients. For example, your operation may have a house specialty that includes an allergen.

Suggest items   Suggest menu items that do not contain the food that the customer is allergic to.

Identify the allergen special order   Clearly mark or otherwise indicate the order for the guest with the identified food allergy, as shown in the photo at left. This is done to inform the kitchen staff of the guest's food allergy.

Deliver food   Confirm the allergen special order with the kitchen staff when picking up the food. Make sure no garnishes or other items containing the allergen touch the plate. Food should be hand-delivered to guests with allergies. Delivering food separately from the other food delivered to a table, as shown in the photo at right, will help prevent contact with food allergens.

Kitchen Staff

Staff must make sure that allergens are not transferred from food or food-contact surfaces containing an allergen to the food served to the customer. This is called cross-contact. Here are examples of how it can happen:

* Cooking different types of food in the same fryer oil. In the photo at right, shrimp allergens could be transferred to the chicken being fried in the same oil.

* Letting food touch surfaces, equipment, or utensils that have touched allergens. For example, putting chocolate chip cookies on the same parchment paper that was used for peanut butter cookies can transfer some of the peanut allergen.

How to Avoid Cross-Contact

* Check recipes and ingredient labels to confirm that the allergen is not present.

* Wash, rinse, and sanitize cookware, utensils, and equipment before prepping food. This includes food-prep surfaces. Some operations use a separate set of cooking utensils just for allergen special orders, as shown in the photo at right.

* Make sure the allergen does not touch anything for customers with food allergies, including food, beverages, utensils, equipment, and gloves.

* Wash your hands and change gloves before prepping food.

* Use separate fryers and cooking oils when frying food for customers with food allergies.

* Label food packaged on-site for retail sale. Name all major allergens on the label and follow any additional labeling requirements.

Apply Your Knowledge

Identify the Symptoms   Write an X next to the symptoms that could indicate a customer is having an allergic reaction.

1 _yes_   **Fever**

2 _yes_   **Hives**

3 _____   **Nausea**

4 _yes_   **Bruising**

5 _yes_   **Sneezing**

6 _____   **Coughing**

7 _____   **Diarrhea**

8 _yes_   **Itchy rash**

9 _____   **Swollen face**

10 _____   **Abdominal pain**

11 _yes_   **Shortness of breath**

12 _yes_   **Tightening in the chest**

For answers, please turn to page 2.34.

Apply Your Knowledge

The Most Common Food Allergens   Write an X next to a food if it is or contains one of the eight most common food allergens.

1. _____ Green beans dressed with olive oil and garlic

2. _____ Smoked salmon wrapped in a lettuce leaf

3. _____ Multigrain bread made with wheat

4. _____ Melon slices wrapped with prosciutto (ham)

5. _____ Chocolate candy filled with peanut butter cream

6. _____ Raw oysters on the half shell

7. _____ Potatoes sautéed in duck fat

8. _____ Mushrooms seasoned with soy sauce and brown sugar

9. _____ Squash sautéed in corn oil

10. _____ Mixed green salad topped with walnut pieces

11. _____ Banana shake made with vanilla ice cream

12. _____ Vegetable omelet topped with tomato sauce

For answers, please turn to page 2.34.

Apply Your Knowledge

Keeping Customers with Allergies Safe   Read each situation and determine whether the employee did the right thing to help prevent an allergic reaction.

1 A customer told Daniel the server that he had a dairy allergy. The customer wanted to know if the chicken salad had any dairy in it. Daniel was honest and told him that he was not totally sure, but it was probably fine.

Did Daniel do the right thing to keep the customer safe? Why or why not?

_____

_____

_____

_____

2 The customer with the dairy allergy then asked about the chicken sandwich. Now Daniel was positive that there was no dairy in that one, so he let him know. The customer ordered the chicken sandwich and fries, and Daniel made sure to note the allergy on the order. The customer's friend ordered a cheeseburger.

Did Daniel do the right thing to keep the customer safe? Why or why not?

_____

_____

_____

_____

3 In the kitchen, Laura the cook noted the allergen special order. She could not remember if the breaded chicken used in the sandwich was dairy-free, so she double-checked the label. Fortunately, it did not have any dairy.

Did Laura do the right thing to keep the customer safe? Why or why not?

_____

_____

_____

_____

Keeping Customers with Allergies Safe *(continued)*

4 Before starting the order, Laura washed, rinsed, and sanitized the prep station and got out clean utensils. Then she washed her hands and put on new gloves. She used the fryer that is only for allergen special orders to cook the chicken and fries. As she finished assembling the sandwich and plating the order, she was careful to use the clean prep station and keep the special order separated from the other orders.

Did Laura do the right thing to keep the customer safe? Why or why not?

_____

_____

_____

_____

5 When the order was ready, Daniel confirmed with the kitchen that it was the allergen special order. He also checked the plate to make sure that there was not anything with any dairy on it. Then he hand-delivered the chicken sandwich order to the customer with the dairy allergy. Another server brought out the cheeseburger for the customer's friend.

Did Daniel do the right thing to keep the customer safe? Why or why not?

_____

_____

_____

_____

For answers, please turn to page 2.34.

Chapter Summary

- Contamination is the presence of harmful substances in food. Those substances can be biological, chemical, or physical.

- Pathogens are disease-causing microorganisms. There are four types that can contaminate food and cause foodborne illness. These are viruses, bacteria, parasites, and fungi. Of the six most common pathogens, four are bacteria and two are viruses.

- Biological contamination occurs when pathogens grow in food. This happens under certain conditions. These conditions can be remembered by the word **FAT TOM**. It stands for food, acidity, temperature, time, oxygen, and moisture. Of these, you will most likely be able to control only time and temperature.

- Viruses require a host to grow. People can get viruses from contaminated food, water, or surfaces. Many viruses are transferred through the fecal-oral route. Most are not destroyed by normal cooking temperatures. The best prevention measures are to purchase food from approved, reputable suppliers and to practice good personal hygiene.

- Parasites require a host to live and reproduce. They are commonly associated with seafood and food processed with contaminated water. The most important measure for preventing parasites from causing a foodborne illness is to purchase food from approved, reputable suppliers.

- Fungi include mold, yeasts, and mushrooms. Like parasites, they are best prevented by purchasing food from approved, reputable suppliers.

- Chemical contamination occurs when chemicals get into food and beverages. Chemical contaminants include toxic metals, cleaners, sanitizers, polishes, and machine lubricants. To help prevent chemical contamination, store chemicals away from prep areas, food storage areas, and service areas. Always follow the manufacturers' directions when using chemicals.

- Physical contamination can happen when objects get into food. Naturally occurring objects, such as bones in a fish fillet, are a physical hazard. Closely inspect the food you receive. Make sure no physical contaminants can get into it at any point during the flow of food.

- People may try to tamper with food using biological, chemical, physical, or even radioactive contaminants. The key to protecting food is to make it hard for someone to tamper with it.

- A food allergen is a naturally occurring protein in a food or ingredient that some people are sensitive to. The most common food allergens include milk, eggs, soy, fish, tree nuts, peanuts, crustacean shellfish, and wheat. Service staff must be able to tell customers about menu items that contain potential allergens. Kitchen staff must make sure that allergens are not transferred from food containing an allergen to the food served to the customer with allergies.

Chapter Review Case Study

Now, take what you have learned in this chapter and apply it to the following case study.

Shawn, the chef at Sunnyside Café, decided to prepare his famous potato salad. After cooking the potatoes, he started to gather all the ingredients to make the potato salad. However, he stopped to run to the restroom, as his stomach was upset. He came back to the kitchen and started prepping the potato salad as the lunch rush would begin soon.

The next day, Sunnyside Café received several complaints of customers with vomiting and diarrhea. Shawn took the callers' information and offered to send them each a coupon for two free meals. Shawn suspected the potato salad was the problem, but all of it had been used the previous day.

Shawn immediately closed the café and threw away any food that had been opened. He also had staff clean and sanitize the prep areas. Then he called an emergency crew meeting to review standards and procedures. Satisfied that he had addressed any problem, he reopened the next day.

1 What did Shawn do right?

_____

_____

_____

_____

2 What did Shawn do wrong?

_____

_____

_____

_____

_____

_____

_____

_____

For answers, please turn to page 2.35.

Study Questions

Circle the best answer to each question.

1 **What are the most common symptoms of a foodborne illness?**

　A　Diarrhea, vomiting, fever, nausea, abdominal cramps, and dizziness

　B　Diarrhea, vomiting, fever, nausea, abdominal cramps, and headache

　C　Diarrhea, vomiting, fever, nausea, abdominal cramps, and jaundice

　D　Diarrhea, vomiting, fever, nausea, abdominal cramps, and tiredness

2 **How does most contamination of food happen?**

　A　Through contaminated water

　B　When contaminants are airborne

　C　When people cause the contamination

　D　Through the use of contaminated animal products

3 **What is the most important way to prevent a foodborne illness from bacteria?**

　A　Control time and temperature.

　B　Prevent cross-contamination.

　C　Practice good personal hygiene.

　D　Practice good cleaning and sanitizing.

4 **What is the most important way to prevent a foodborne illness from viruses?**

　A　Control time and temperature.

　B　Prevent cross-contamination.

　C　Practice good personal hygiene.

　D　Practice good cleaning and sanitizing.

5 **Parasites are commonly linked with what type of food?**

　A　Rice

　B　Poultry

　C　Seafood

　D　Canned food

Study Questions

6 **A guest had a reversal of hot and cold sensations after eating seafood. What most likely caused the illness?**

A   Parasites

B   Allergic reaction

C   Biological toxins

D   Chemical contamination

7 **A prep cook stores a bottle of sanitizer on a shelf above a prep table. To prevent chemical contamination, what should be done differently?**

A   Store the sanitizer bottle away from the prep area.

B   Store the sanitizer bottle on the floor between uses.

C   Store the sanitizer bottle on the work surface of the prep table.

D   Store the sanitizer bottle with food supplies below the prep table.

8 **To prevent the deliberate contamination of food, a manager should know who is in the facility, monitor the security of products, keep information related to food security on file, and know**

A   when to register with the EPA.

B   how to fill out an incident report.

C   where to find Safety Data Sheets in the operation.

D   whom to contact about suspicious activity.

9 **What should food handlers do to prevent food allergens from being transferred to food?**

A   Use clean and sanitized utensils when prepping the order.

B   Cook food to the appropriate minimum internal temperature.

C   Store cold food at 41°F (5°C) or lower.

D   Label chemical containers correctly.

10 **What step should be taken if a manager suspects a foodborne-illness outbreak?**

A   Reheat the suspected product to safe temperatures.

B   Provide as little information as possible to the regulatory authority.

C   Deny that the operation has anything to do with the foodborne-illness outbreak.

D   Set aside the suspected product and label it with "do not use" and "do not discard."

For answers, please turn to page 2.35.

Answers

2.12   Which Ones Are Contaminants?

1, 2, and 3 should be marked. The food handler is pulling out bones from a fish fillet in photo 1. The cherry pit in photo 2 could be mixed with the final dish. The container of Chinese food in photo 3 has been stapled shut. The staple can easily end up in the food.

2.13   What's Wrong with This Picture?

1 and 2 should be marked. The chemicals in photo 1 are being stored with food. The food handler spraying chemicals near the fryer oil could contaminate the oil in photo 2. The food handler in photo 3 is using the spray sanitizer correctly.

2.13   What's It Stand For?

1 Food

2 Acidity

3 Temperature

4 Time

5 Oxygen

6 Moisture

2.14   Who Am I?

1 Hepatitis A

2 *Salmonella* Typhi

3 Nontyphoidal *Salmonella*

Answers

2.15   What's the Best Way to Control Them?

1 A

2 B

3 C

4 C

5 C

6 C

7 C

2.17   The Best Defense

2, 4, 5, 7, and 8 should be marked.

2.19   Handling a Foodborne-Illness Outbreak

1 What did Emma do right?

   - She gathered detailed information from the customers who called.

   - She notified the local regulatory authority of the suspected outbreak.

   - She identified staff who were scheduled at the time of the suspected contamination.

2 What did Emma do wrong?

   - She threw away the suspected product rather than segregating it.

   - She failed to document information about the suspected product.

Answers

2.24 Identify the Symptoms

2, 3, 7, 8, 9, 10, and 11 should be marked.

2.25 The Most Common Food Allergens

2, 3, 5, 6, 8, 10, 11, and 12 should be marked.

2.26 Keeping Customers with Allergies Safe

1 No. Daniel should not have guessed about the ingredients. Servers must be able to describe how a dish is prepared. Servers should also be able to suggest menu items that they are certain do not have food allergens.

2 Yes. Daniel was able to confirm that there was no dairy in the item. He also clearly identified the allergen special order on the order ticket.

3 Yes. Laura checked the ingredient label to confirm that the breaded chicken did not contain any dairy.

4 Yes. Laura washed, rinsed, and sanitized the equipment before preparing the order. She used the fryer designated for allergy special orders. She made sure that no dairy touched the order as she was prepping it.

5 Yes. First, he checked with the kitchen staff to make sure he was getting the allergen special order. Then he made sure that the plate did not have any garnishes or other items containing the allergen. He also hand-delivered the allergen special order to the guest, and this was done separately from the other food to prevent contact with allergens.

Answers

2.29 Chapter Review Case Study

1 What did Shawn do right?

- He got the customers' contact information and information about their experiences.

- He reviewed standards and procedures with his staff.

2 What did Shawn do wrong?

- He bought food from a supplier without first checking the supplier's credentials.

- He did not wash his hands before handling the eggs and again before handling the toast, orange slices, and plates of food.

- He failed to document information about the suspected product.

- He failed to notify the local regulatory authority of the suspected outbreak.

- He failed to identify staff who may have been in contact with the suspected product.

2.30 Study Questions

1 C

2 C

3 A

4 C

5 C

6 C

7 A

8 D

9 A

10 D

How Food Handlers Can Contaminate Food

At every step in the flow of food, food handlers can contaminate food. They might not even realize it when they do it. Something as simple as touching the face while prepping a salad could make a customer sick. Even a food handler who appears to be healthy may spread foodborne pathogens. As a manager, you need to know the many ways that food handlers can contaminate food.

Situations That Can Lead to Contaminating Food

Food handlers can contaminate food in any of the following situations:

- When they have a foodborne illness.

- When they have wounds or boils that contain a pathogen.

- When sneezing or coughing, as the food handler is doing in the photo at left.

- When they have contact with a person who is ill.

- When they use the restroom and do not wash their hands. These food handlers may contaminate food and surfaces with feces from their fingers. Once someone eats food contaminated this way, a foodborne illness may result. This is called the fecal-oral route of contamination.

- When they have symptoms such as diarrhea, vomiting, or jaundice—a yellowing of the eyes or skin.

With some illnesses, a person may infect other people before showing any symptoms. For example, a person could spread Hepatitis A for weeks before having any symptoms. With other illnesses, a person may infect other people for days or even months after symptoms are gone. Norovirus can be spread for days after symptoms have ended.

Some people carry pathogens and infect others without ever getting sick themselves. These people are called carriers.

Actions That Can Contaminate Food

To avoid causing a foodborne illness, pay close attention to what you do with your hands. Some common actions to avoid are:

A   Scratching the scalp

B   Running fingers through the hair

C   Wiping or touching the nose

D   Rubbing an ear

E   Touching a pimple or an infected wound/boil

F   Wearing and touching a dirty uniform

G   Coughing or sneezing into the hand

H   Spitting in the operation

Managing a Personal Hygiene Program

To keep food handlers from contaminating food, your operation needs a good personal hygiene program. A good personal hygiene program also helps everyone feel confident in the cleanliness of the business. As a manager, you must make sure this program succeeds.

Do not underestimate your role in a personal hygiene program. You have a responsibility to create the program and make sure it works. Some things to support a personal hygiene program include:

- Creating personal hygiene policies.

- Training food handlers on those policies and retraining them regularly.

- Modeling the correct behavior at all times. The manager in the photo at right is modeling good personal hygiene practices. He is wearing clean clothes and a hair restraint. He is also using gloves.

- Supervising food safety practices at all times.

- Revising personal hygiene policies when laws or science change.

Apply Your Knowledge

Who Is at Risk? Write an X next to the food handler whose actions could spread pathogens.

1 _____

2 _____

3 _____

4 _____

For answers, please turn to page 3.24.

Handwashing and Hand Care

Proper handwashing and hand care are critical to preventing the spread of pathogens.

Handwashing

Handwashing is the most important part of personal hygiene. And many food handlers do not wash their hands correctly or as often as they should. Every day our hands touch surfaces covered with microorganisms that we cannot see. Even healthy people can spread pathogens. You must train your food handlers to wash their hands, and then you must monitor them.

Where to Wash Hands

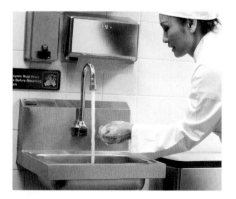

Hands must be washed in a sink designated for handwashing. Monitor food handlers to make sure they do this. They should **NEVER** wash their hands in sinks designated for food prep or dishwashing or sinks used for discarding waste water. The food handler in the photo at left is using a designated handwashing sink.

How to Wash Hands

To wash hands or prosthetic devices correctly, follow these steps. The whole process should take at least 20 seconds.

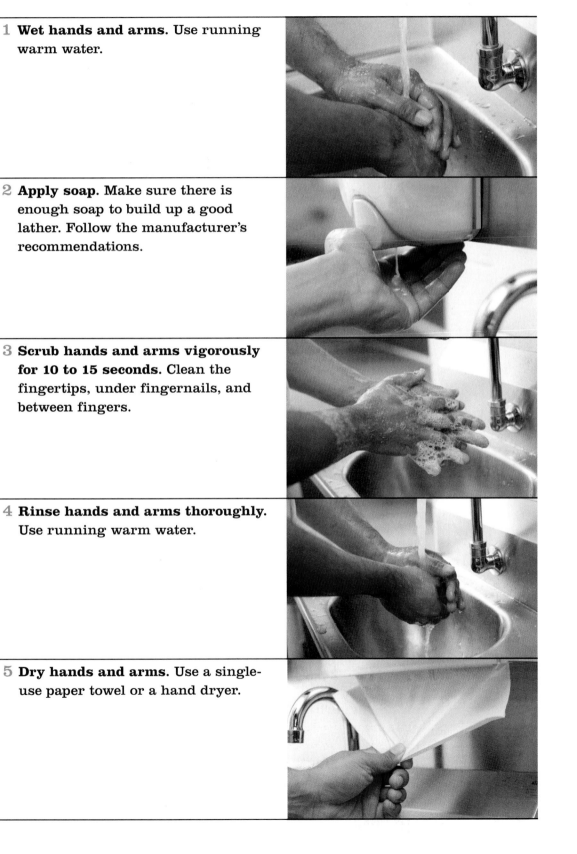

1 **Wet hands and arms.** Use running warm water.

2 **Apply soap.** Make sure there is enough soap to build up a good lather. Follow the manufacturer's recommendations.

3 **Scrub hands and arms vigorously for 10 to 15 seconds.** Clean the fingertips, under fingernails, and between fingers.

4 **Rinse hands and arms thoroughly.** Use running warm water.

5 **Dry hands and arms.** Use a single-use paper towel or a hand dryer.

If you are not careful, you can contaminate your hands after washing them. Consider using a paper towel to turn off the faucet and to open the door when leaving the restroom. The food handler in the photo at left is using a paper towel to open the restroom door in order to avoid contamination.

When to Wash Hands

Food handlers must wash their hands before preparing food or working with clean equipment and utensils. They must also wash their hands before putting on single-use gloves. The buser pictured below washed his hands before unloading the clean glasses.

Food handlers must wash their hands after the following activities:

- Using the restroom.
- Touching the body or clothing.
- Coughing, sneezing, blowing nose, or using a handkerchief or tissue.
- Eating, drinking, smoking, or chewing gum or tobacco.
- Handling soiled items.
- Handling raw meat, seafood, or poultry.
- Taking out garbage.

- Handling service animals or aquatic animals.

- Handling chemicals that might affect food safety.

- Changing tasks (before beginning new task).

- Leaving and returning to the kitchen/prep area.

- Handling money.

- Using electronic devices. The food handler in the photo at right must wash his hands before working with food or clean equipment and utensils.

- Touching anything else that may contaminate hands, such as dirty equipment, work surfaces, or cloths.

Corrective Action

If you see food handlers who are not following proper handwashing procedures, correct the situation immediately. If they have touched food or food-contact surfaces with unclean hands:

- Dispose of the contaminated food.

- Clean potentially contaminated equipment and utensils.

- Retrain or coach food handlers who are not following proper handwashing procedures if necessary.

Hand Antiseptics

Hand antiseptics, also called hand sanitizers, are liquids or gels that are used to lower the number of pathogens on skin. If used, they must comply with the Code of Federal Regulations (CFR) and Food and Drug Administration (FDA) standards.

Only use hand antiseptics after handwashing. **NEVER** use them in place of it. Wait for a hand antiseptic to dry before you touch food or equipment.

Hand Care

In addition to washing, hands need other care to prevent spreading pathogens. Make sure food handlers follow the guidelines in Table 3.1 on the next page.

Table 3.1: **Hand-Care Guidelines**

Topic	Guidelines
✓	**Fingernail length** Keep fingernails short and clean. Long fingernails may be hard to keep clean and can rip gloves. They can also chip and become physical contaminants. Fingernails should be kept trimmed and filed. This will allow nails to be cleaned easily. Ragged nails can be hard to keep clean. They may also hold pathogens and break off—becoming physical contaminants.
⊘	**False fingernails** Do **NOT** wear false fingernails. They can be hard to keep clean. False fingernails also can break off into food. However, false fingernails can be worn if the food handler wears single-use gloves.
⊘	**Nail polish** Do **NOT** wear nail polish. It can disguise dirt under nails and may flake off into food. However, nail polish can be worn if the food handler wears single-use gloves.

Infected wounds or boils

Infected wounds, cuts, and boils contain pus. They must be covered if they are open or draining to prevent pathogens from contaminating food and food-contact surfaces. How an infected wound or boil is covered depends on where it is located.

✓	If the wound or boil is located on the hand or wrist	Then cover it with an impermeable cover like a finger cot. **Impermeable** means that liquid cannot pass through the cover. Examples include bandages and finger cots. Place a single-use glove over the cover.
✓	If the wound or boil is located on the arm	Then cover it with an impermeable cover, such as a bandage. The wound must be completely covered.
✓	If the wound or boil is located on another part of the body	Then cover it with a dry, durable, tight-fitting bandage.

Apply Your Knowledge

When to Wash Hands?   Write an X next to the statement if the food handler washed his or her hands at the correct time.

1 _____ Linda prepped raw chicken for the day's special. Then she washed her hands and sliced melons. After that, she washed and sanitized the cutting boards.

2 _____ Ryan was busing tables when his manager asked him to take out the garbage. When he came back, he used the restroom and washed his hands. Then he set up some tables.

3 _____ Maria was making meatballs when she took a call on her mobile phone. Her manager was nearby, so she quickly got back to work. Afterward, she wiped down her phone and washed her hands.

4 _____ Caitlyn started a batch of French fries in the fryer. While they were cooking, she took two orders at the cash register. As soon as the fries were done, she salted and packaged them. Then she washed her hands and packed the customers' orders.

Is That Right?   Write an X next to the statement if the food handler correctly followed hand-care guidelines and handwashing procedures.

1 _____ Gabe, a restaurant manager, noticed that prep cooks were washing their hands in the prep sink. Gabe immediately spoke to the employees about designated hand sinks and appropriate versus inappropriate locations for washing hands.

2 _____ Michael plated an order and leafed through the paper tickets to make sure he had it right. Before touching each ticket, he licked his fingers to get a better grip. Fortunately, he realized his mistake. He quickly applied hand antiseptic and then ran the order to the table.

3 _____ Tina had a painful paper cut on her index finger. She liked it to be exposed to air so it would heal quickly. But at work, she covered it with a waterproof bandage and wore a finger cot.

4 _____ Marcus saw his dish washer, John, sneeze into his hands and then begin to put away clean dishes. Marcus stopped John and asked him to wash his hands. Then he had John put all the contaminated dishes back into the dishwashing machine. Afterward, Marcus worked with John to make sure he knew when to wash his hands.

5 _____ Carmen just finished food safety training and is eager to do the right thing. To wash her hands, she first applied soap. Then she used a clean paper towel to turn on the warm water. She wet her hands and arms and scrubbed them for five seconds. Afterward, she rinsed them thoroughly and dried them with a clean paper towel.

For answers, please turn to page 3.24.

Single-Use Gloves

Many operations use single-use gloves when handling food. As the name implies, single-use gloves are designed for one task, after which they must be discarded. Used properly, they can help keep food safe by creating a barrier between hands and food. However, single-use gloves should **NEVER** be used in place of handwashing.

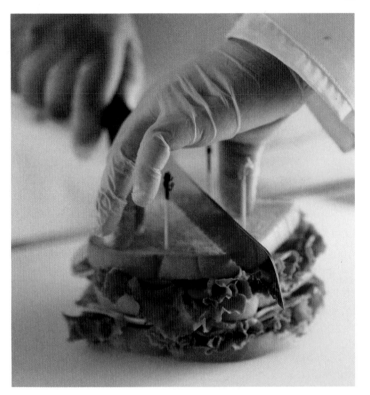

Single-use gloves should always be worn when handling ready-to-eat food, as shown in the photo at left. The exceptions include when washing produce or when handling ready-to-eat ingredients for a dish that will be cooked to the correct internal temperature.

Which Gloves to Buy

When buying gloves for handling food, follow these guidelines.

Approved gloves   Only gloves approved for foodservice should be purchased.

Disposable gloves   Buy only single-use gloves for handling food. **NEVER** wash and reuse gloves.

Multiple sizes   Make sure you provide different glove sizes.

Latex alternatives   Some food handlers and customers may be sensitive to latex. Consider providing gloves made from other materials.

Something to Think About

At an operation on the East Coast, the salad bar was very popular. One afternoon while prepping lettuce, a food handler cut her finger. She bandaged it right away, but she did not wear gloves. While she was tossing the salad, her bandage fell off into it. Soon after, a customer reported that she had found the used bandage in her salad. The manager quickly apologized and comped the customer's meal.

How to Use Gloves

When using single-use gloves, follow these guidelines to prevent contamination:

- Wash your hands before putting on gloves when starting a new task. You do not need to rewash your hands each time you change gloves as long as you are performing the same task and your hands have not become contaminated.

- Select the correct glove size. Gloves that are too big will not stay on. Those that are too small will tear or rip easily. The photo at right shows a correct fit.

- Hold gloves by the edge when putting them on. Avoid touching the glove as much as possible.

- Once you have put them on, check the gloves for rips or tears.

- **NEVER** blow into gloves.

- **NEVER** roll gloves to make them easier to put on.

- **NEVER** wash and reuse gloves.

When to Change Gloves

Food handlers must change single-use gloves at all of these times:

- As soon as the gloves become dirty or torn.

- Before beginning a different task.

- After an interruption, such as taking a phone call.

- After handling raw meat, seafood, or poultry, and before handling ready-to-eat food.

- After four hours of continuous use.

Bare-Hand Contact with Ready-to-Eat Food

Food can become contaminated when it has been handled with bare hands. This is especially true when hands have not been washed correctly or have infected cuts or wounds. For this reason, do **NOT** handle ready-to-eat food with bare hands. And, if you primarily serve a high-risk population, **NEVER** handle ready-to-eat food with bare hands.

However, there may be exceptions. It may be acceptable to handle ready-to-eat food with bare hands in these situations:

- The food will be added as an ingredient to a dish that does not contain raw meat, seafood, or poultry, but will be cooked to at least 145°F (63°C). For example, adding cheese to pizza dough.

- The food will be added as an ingredient to a dish containing raw meat, seafood, or poultry, and the dish will be cooked to the required minimum internal temperature of the raw items. For example, adding salt and pepper to raw duck breasts, as shown in the photo at left.

Some regulatory authorities allow bare-hand contact with ready-to-eat food. If your jurisdiction allows this, you must have specific policies in place about staff health. You must also train staff in handwashing and personal hygiene practices.

Apply Your Knowledge

When to Use Single-Use Gloves   Write an X next to the task when single-use gloves must be used.

1 _____ Slicing apples for an apple pie.

2 _____ Garnishing a plate with chopped herbs.

3 _____ Chopping lettuce for a mixed green salad.

4 _____ Breading chicken wings before frying them.

5 _____ Assembling a cooked hamburger for presentation.

For answers, please turn to page 3.24.

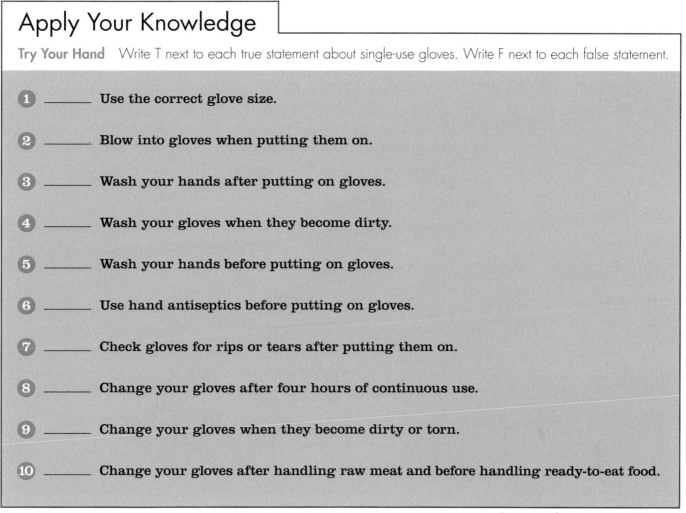

Apply Your Knowledge

Try Your Hand   Write T next to each true statement about single-use gloves. Write F next to each false statement.

1. _____ Use the correct glove size.

2. _____ Blow into gloves when putting them on.

3. _____ Wash your hands after putting on gloves.

4. _____ Wash your gloves when they become dirty.

5. _____ Wash your hands before putting on gloves.

6. _____ Use hand antiseptics before putting on gloves.

7. _____ Check gloves for rips or tears after putting them on.

8. _____ Change your gloves after four hours of continuous use.

9. _____ Change your gloves when they become dirty or torn.

10. _____ Change your gloves after handling raw meat and before handling ready-to-eat food.

For answers, please turn to page 3.24.

Personal Hygiene Practices

Wearing dirty clothes or neglecting to shower probably will not go over well with your guests. But there are real food safety concerns, too. Keeping food safe means paying attention to personal hygiene. The entire staff needs to know the basics.

Personal Cleanliness

Pathogens can be found on hair and skin. There is a greater risk of these pathogens being transferred to food and food equipment if the food handler does not follow a personal hygiene program. Make sure food handlers shower or bathe before work.

Work Attire

Food handlers in dirty clothes may give a bad impression of your operation. More important, dirty clothing may carry pathogens that can cause foodborne illnesses. These pathogens can be transferred from the clothing to the hands and to the food being prepared. Set up a dress code, and make sure all staff follow it. The code should include the guidelines listed in Table 3.2, on the next page.

Eating, Drinking, Smoking, and Chewing Gum or Tobacco

Small droplets of saliva can contain thousands of pathogens. In the process of eating, drinking, smoking, or chewing gum or tobacco, saliva can be transferred to hands or directly to food being handled.

To prevent this, employees should only eat, drink, smoke, and chew gum or tobacco in designated areas. **NEVER** do these things when:

- Prepping or serving food
- Working in prep areas
- Working in areas used to clean utensils and equipment

Employees can drink from a covered container if they handle the container carefully to prevent contamination of their hands, the container, and exposed food, utensils, and equipment. A correctly covered container will include a lid with a straw, or a sip-lid top. The chef in the photo at left is using the correct container and lid.

Table 3.2: **Work Attire Guidelines**

Attire	Guidelines
	**Hair restraints** • Wear a clean hat or other hair restraint when in a food-prep area. This can keep hair from falling into food and onto food-contact surfaces. • Do **NOT** wear hair accessories that could become physical contaminants. Hair accessories should be limited to items that keep hands out of hair and hair out of food. • Do **NOT** wear false eyelashes. They can become physical contaminants. • Food handlers with facial hair should also wear a beard restraint.
	Clean clothing • Wear clean clothing daily. • Change soiled uniforms, including aprons, as needed to prevent contamination. • If possible, change into work clothes at work. • Store street clothing and personal belongings in designated areas. This includes items such as backpacks, jackets, electronic devices, keys, and personal medications. Make sure these items are stored in a way that does not contaminate food, food-contact surfaces, and linens. • Keep dirty clothing that is stored in the operation away from food and prep areas. You can do this by placing dirty clothes in nonabsorbent containers or washable laundry bags. This includes dirty aprons, chef coats, and other uniforms.
	Aprons • Remove aprons when leaving prep areas. For example, aprons should be removed and stored before taking out garbage or using the restroom. • **NEVER** wipe your hands on your apron.

	Jewelry
	• Remove jewelry from hands and arms before prepping food or when working around prep areas. Food handlers cannot wear any of the following:
	  • Rings, except for a plain band
	  • Bracelets, including medical bracelets
	  • Watches
	• Your company may also require you to remove other types of jewelry. This may include earrings, necklaces, and facial jewelry. These items can fall off and become a physical contaminant. Ornate jewelry can be difficult to clean and can hold pathogens. Servers may wear jewelry if allowed by company policy.

Apply Your Knowledge

What Is Wrong with This Picture?   Write an X next to each photo that shows a hygiene problem.

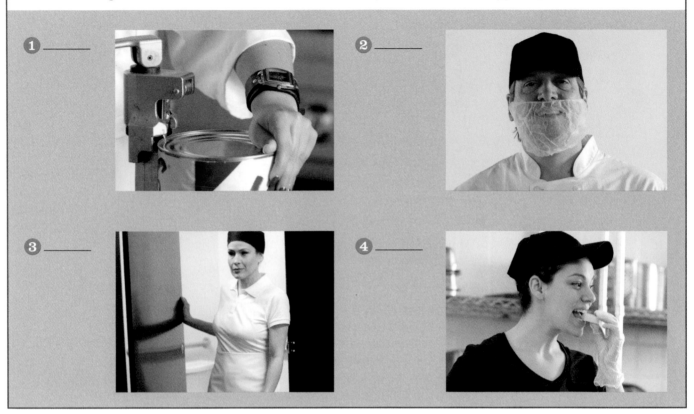

1 _____

2 _____

3 _____

4 _____

For answers, please turn to page 3.24.

Policies for Reporting Health Issues

You must tell your staff to let you know when they are sick. This includes newly hired staff who have not started working yet. Your regulatory authority may ask for proof that you have done this, which can be provided in the following ways:

- Presenting signed statements in which staff have agreed to report illness

- Providing documentation showing staff have completed training, which includes information on the importance of reporting illness

- Posting signs or providing pocket cards that remind staff to notify managers when they are sick

Reporting Illness

Staff must report illnesses before they come to work. They should also let you know immediately if they get sick while working, as the food handler in the photo shown at right is doing.

When food handlers are sick, you may need to restrict them from working with exposed food, utensils, and equipment. Sometimes you may even need to exclude sick employees from coming into the operation. This is especially important if they have these symptoms:

- Vomiting
- Diarrhea
- Jaundice (a yellowing of the skin or eyes)
- Sore throat with fever
- Infected wound or boil that is open or draining (unless properly covered)

Staff must also tell you when they have been diagnosed with an illness from one of these pathogens:

- Norovirus
- Hepatitis A
- *Shigella* spp.
- Shiga-toxin producing *E. coli* (STEC)
- *Salmonella* Typhi
- Nontyphoidal *Salmonella*

They must also tell you if they live with someone who has been diagnosed with any of these illnesses, except nontyphoidal *Salmonella*.

If a food handler is diagnosed with an illness from any of these pathogens, you must report the illness to your regulatory authority. See Table 3.3 for more information.

Watching for Staff Illnesses

As a manager, you should watch food handlers for signs of illness. That could include watching for things like:

- Vomiting
- Excessive trips to the bathroom
- Yellowing of the skin, eyes, and fingernails
- Cold sweats or chills (indicating a fever)
- Persistent nasal discharge and sneezing

Restricting or Excluding Staff for Medical Conditions

Use the following chart to help you decide how to handle staff illnesses and other medical conditions that can affect food safety. Note that for most illnesses, however, you should work with your local regulatory authority to determine how to respond.

Table 3.3: How to Handle Medical Conditions

If	Then
The food handler has an infected wound or boil that is not properly covered.	**Restrict** the food handler from working with exposed food, utensils, and equipment.
The food handler has a sore throat with a fever.	**Restrict** the food handler from working with exposed food, utensils, and equipment. **Exclude** the food handler from the operation if you primarily serve a high-risk population. The food handler can return to the operation and/or work with or around food when he or she has a written release from a medical practitioner.
The food handler has persistent sneezing, coughing, or a runny nose that causes discharges from the eyes, nose, or mouth.	**Restrict** the food handler from working with exposed food, utensils, and equipment.
The food handler has at least one of these symptoms from an infectious condition: • Vomiting • Diarrhea • Jaundice (yellow skin or eyes)	**Exclude** the food handler from the operation. **Vomiting and diarrhea** Food handlers must meet one of these requirements before they can return to work: • Have had no symptoms for at least 24 hours. • Have a written release from a medical practitioner. **Jaundice** Food handlers with jaundice must be reported to the regulatory authority. Food handlers who have had jaundice for seven days or less must be excluded from the operation. Food handlers must have a written release from a medical practitioner and approval from the regulatory authority before returning to work.

Table 3.3: **How to Handle Medical Conditions** *(continued)*

If	Then
The food handler is vomiting or has diarrhea and has been diagnosed with an illness caused by one of these pathogens: • Norovirus • *Shigella* spp. • Nontyphoidal *Salmonella* • Shiga toxin-producing *E. coli* (STEC) The food handler has been diagnosed with an illness caused by one of these pathogens: • Hepatitis A • *Salmonella* Typhi	**Exclude** the food handler from the operation. **Report** the situation to the regulatory authority. Some food handlers diagnosed with an illness may not experience symptoms, or their symptoms may have ended. Work with the medical practitioner and the local regulatory authority to determine whether the food handlers must be excluded from the operation or restricted from working with exposed food, utensils, and equipment. The medical practitioner and regulatory authority will also determine when the employees can safely return to the operation and/or carry out their regular food handling duties.

This chart is only a guide. Work with your local regulatory authority to determine the best course of action.

Apply Your Knowledge

Exclusion or Restriction?   Write an E next to the statement if the food handler must be excluded from the operation. Write an R next to the statement if the person should be restricted from working with exposed food, utensils, and equipment.

1. _____ Joe, a prep cook, has diarrhea.

2. _____ Louisa, a buser, has a runny nose.

3. _____ Bill, a line cook in a restaurant, has a sore throat with a fever.

4. _____ Mary, a sous chef, has been diagnosed with Norovirus.

For answers, please turn to page 3.25.

Chapter Summary

- Food handlers can spread pathogens and contaminate food at every step in the flow of food. Good personal hygiene is critical in preventing contamination.

- Food handlers pose a greater risk for contaminating food when they have a foodborne illness; wounds or boils that contain a pathogen; contact with someone who is sick; or symptoms such as sneezing, coughing, diarrhea, vomiting, or jaundice. The risk is also greater when food handlers use the restroom and do not wash their hands.

- Other common ways that food handlers can contaminate food include touching the scalp, hair, nose, or ears; touching a pimple or wound; wearing and touching a dirty uniform; coughing or sneezing into their hand; and spitting in the operation.

- Hands must be cared for and washed correctly. They must be washed at a sink designated for handwashing. They also must be washed at the correct times. This includes before preparing food, working with clean equipment and utensils, putting on single-use gloves, and starting a new task. Food handlers must also wash hands after using the restroom and after many other activities that can contaminate their hands. Hand antiseptics should never be used in place of handwashing.

- If you see that food handlers have not washed their hands correctly and have touched food or food-contact surfaces, you must take corrective action immediately. Dispose of the contaminated food. Clean equipment and utensils that may have been contaminated. As needed, retrain or coach employees on handwashing.

- Single-use gloves must be worn when handling ready-to-eat food. Wash hands before putting on gloves. Wear the right size glove. Avoid touching the gloves when you put them on. Change your gloves when they are dirty or torn; before starting a new task; after an interruption in your task; after handling raw meat, seafood, or poultry and before handling ready-to-eat food; and after four hours of continuous use. Never handle ready-to-eat food with bare hands if you primarily serve a high-risk population.

- Before handling food or working in prep areas, food handlers must put on clean clothing and a clean hair restraint. They must remove jewelry from hands and arms. Aprons should be removed and stored when food handlers leave prep areas.

- Food handlers should only eat, smoke, or chew gum or tobacco in designated areas. They may drink from a covered container that has a lid and straw or a sip-lid top if they are careful to prevent contamination.

- Staff must report health problems to management before working with food. Managers should also watch for staff illnesses. Food handlers must be excluded from work if they are vomiting or have diarrhea and have been diagnosed with a foodborne illness from certain pathogens, such as nontyphoidal *Salmonella*. Food handlers also must not come to work if they have symptoms that include diarrhea, vomiting, or jaundice. Staff who have persistent sneezing, coughing, or a runny nose or a sore throat and a fever should not work with exposed food, utensils, or equipment. Check with your regulatory authority for requirements that apply to your operation.

- To keep food handlers from contaminating food, your operation needs a good personal hygiene program. You can minimize the risk of foodborne illnesses by establishing a program, training staff, and enforcing the program. Most important, you must set an example yourself by practicing good personal hygiene.

Chapter Review Case Study

You can avoid spreading pathogens to food if you follow a good personal hygiene program. This includes avoiding personal behaviors that can contaminate food; washing and caring for hands; following a dress code; limiting where food handlers can eat, drink, smoke, and chew gum or tobacco; and preventing food handlers who may be carrying pathogens from working with or around food or, if necessary, excluding them from the operation.

Now, take what you have learned in this chapter and apply it to the following case study.

Robert is a food handler at a deli. It is 7:47 a.m., and he has just woken up. He is scheduled to be at work and ready to go by 8:00 a.m. When he gets out of bed, his stomach feels queasy. He blames that on the beer he had the night before. Fortunately, Robert lives only five minutes from work. Despite this, he does not have enough time to take a shower. He grabs the same uniform he wore the day before when prepping chicken. He also puts on his watch and several rings.

When Robert gets to work, he realizes that he has left his hat at home. Robert is greeted by an angry manager. The manager puts Robert to work right away, loading the rotisserie with raw chicken. Robert then moves on to serving a customer who orders a freshly made salad. Robert is known for his salads and makes the salad to the customer's approval.

1 Robert made several errors. Identify as many as you can on the lines below.

_____

_____

_____

_____

_____

_____

_____

_____

_____

_____

For answers, please turn to page 3.25.

Study Questions

Circle the best answer to each question.

1 **After which activity must food handlers wash their hands?**

   A   Clearing tables

   B   Putting on gloves

   C   Serving customers

   D   Applying hand antiseptic

2 **When washing hands, what is the minimum time you should scrub with soap?**

   A   5 seconds

   B   10 seconds

   C   20 seconds

   D   40 seconds

3 **What should food handlers do after prepping food and before using the restroom?**

   A   Wash their hands

   B   Take off their hats

   C   Change their gloves

   D   Take off their aprons

4 **A food handler will be wearing single-use gloves to assemble boxed lunches. When must the food handler's hands be washed?**

   A   After 4 hours

   B   After the first hour

   C   After putting on the gloves

   D   Before putting on the gloves

5 **A cook wore single-use gloves while forming raw ground beef into patties. The cook continued to wear them while slicing hamburger buns. What mistake was made?**

   A   The cook did not wear reusable gloves while handling the raw ground beef and hamburger buns.

   B   The cook did not clean and sanitize the gloves before handling the hamburger buns.

   C   The cook did not wash hands before putting on the same gloves to slice the hamburger buns.

   D   The cook did not wash hands and put on new gloves before slicing the hamburger buns.

Study Questions

6 **Who is most at risk of contaminating food?**

A   A food handler whose spouse works primarily with high-risk populations

B   A food handler whose young daughter has diarrhea

C   A food handler who gets a lot of aches and pains

D   A food handler who eats a lot of rare meat

7 **A food handler has diarrhea and has been diagnosed with an illness from *Shigella* spp. What should the manager tell this food handler to do?**

A   Wear gloves while handling food

B   Work in a non-food handling position

C   Stay home until approved to return to work

D   Wash hands frequently while handling food

8 **A food handler prepares meals for a child day-care center. What symptoms require this food handler to stay home from work?**

A   Thirst with itching

B   Soreness with fatigue

C   Sore throat with fever

D   Headache with soreness

9 **When is it acceptable to eat in an operation?**

A   When prepping food

B   When washing dishes

C   When sitting in a break area

D   When handling utensils

10 **What should a manager of a hospital cafeteria do if a cook calls in with a headache, nausea, and diarrhea?**

A   Tell the cook to stay away from work and see a doctor

B   Tell the cook to come in for a couple of hours and then go home

C   Tell the cook to rest for a couple of hours and then come to work

D   Tell the cook to go to the doctor and then immediately come to work

For answers, please turn to page 3.25.

Answers

3.4   Who Is at Risk?

2 and 3 should be marked.

3.9   When to Wash Hands?

1 and 2 should be marked.

3.9   Is That Right?

1, 3, and 4 should be marked.

3.12   When to Use Single-Use Gloves

2, 3, and 5 should be marked.

3.13   Try Your Hand

1 T
2 F
3 F
4 F
5 T
6 F
7 T
8 T
9 T
10 T

3.16   What Is Wrong with This Picture?

1, 3, and 4 should be marked.

Answers

3.19   Exclusion or Restriction?

1 E

2 R

3 R

4 E

3.21   Chapter Review Case Study

Robert made the following errors:

- Robert did not take a bath or shower before work.

- Robert wore a dirty uniform to work.

- Robert should have removed his watch and rings (with the exception of a plain band) before prepping and serving food.

- Robert did not wear a hair restraint.

- Robert did not report his illness to the manager before coming to work.

- Robert did not wash his hands before handling the raw chicken.

- Robert did not wash his hands after handling the raw chicken.

3.22   Study Questions

1 A

2 B

3 D

4 D

5 D

6 B

7 C

8 C

9 C

10 A

Service   Purchasing

Reheating

Receiving

Cooling

FLOW OF FOOD

Storing

Holding

Preparation

Cooking

Hazards in the Flow of Food

To keep food safe, you must apply what you learn in the ServSafe program throughout the flow of food. This is the path that food takes through your operation, as shown in the image at left. It begins when you buy the food and ends when you serve it. Detailed practices for each phase are covered in later chapters.

You are responsible for the safety of the food at every point in this flow—and many things can happen to it.

For example, a frozen food might be safe when it leaves the processor's plant. However, on the way to the supplier's warehouse, the food might thaw. Once in your operation, the food might not be stored correctly, or it might not be cooked to the correct internal temperature. These mistakes can add up and cause a foodborne illness. That is why it is important to understand how to prevent time-temperature abuse and cross-contamination.

Cross-Contamination

Pathogens can move around easily in your operation. They can be spread from food or unwashed hands to prep areas, equipment, utensils, or other food.

Cross-contamination can happen at almost any point in the flow of food. When you know how and where it can happen, it is fairly easy to prevent. The most basic way is to keep raw and ready-to-eat food away from each other. Table 4.1 shows some guidelines for doing this.

Time-Temperature Control

Most foodborne illnesses happen because TCS food has been time-temperature abused. Remember, TCS food has been time-temperature abused any time it remains between 41°F and 135°F (5°C and 57°C). This is called the temperature danger zone because pathogens grow in this range. But most pathogens grow much faster between 70°F and 125°F (21°C and 52°C). These ranges are shown in the image at left. Food is being temperature abused whenever it is handled in the following ways:

- Cooked to the wrong internal temperature
- Held at the wrong temperature
- Cooled or reheated incorrectly

The longer food stays in the temperature danger zone, the more time pathogens have to grow. To keep food safe, you must reduce the time it spends in this temperature range. If food is held in this range for four or more hours, you must throw it out.

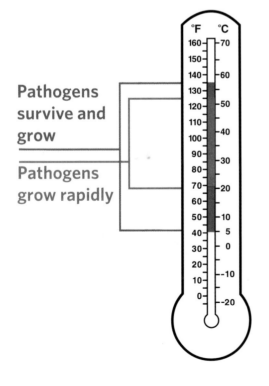

Pathogens survive and grow

Pathogens grow rapidly

Table 4.1: Guidelines for Preventing Cross-Contamination between Food

Guideline	Description
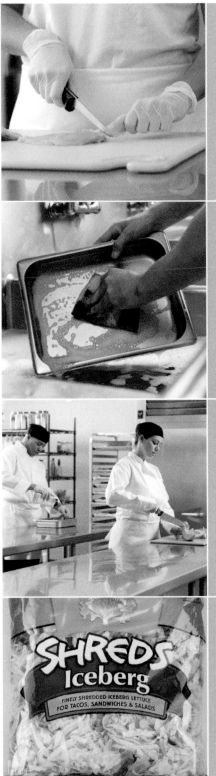	**Use separate equipment for raw and ready-to-eat food** Each type of food should have separate equipment. For example, use one set of cutting boards, utensils, and containers for raw poultry. Use another set for raw meat. Use a third set for produce. Colored cutting boards and utensil handles can help keep equipment separate. The color tells food handlers which equipment to use with each food item. You might use yellow for raw chicken, red for raw meat, and green for produce.
	Clean and sanitize before and after tasks Clean and sanitize all work surfaces, equipment, and utensils before and after each task. When you cut up raw chicken, for example, you cannot get by with just rinsing the equipment. Pathogens such as nontyphoidal *Salmonella* can contaminate food through cross-contamination. To prevent this, you must wash, rinse, and sanitize equipment. See chapter 10 for more information on cleaning and sanitizing.
	Prep raw and ready-to-eat food at different times If you need to use the same prep table for different types of food, prep raw meat, fish, and poultry at a different time than ready-to-eat food. You must clean and sanitize work surfaces and utensils between each type of food. Also, by prepping ready-to-eat food before raw food, you can reduce the chance for cross-contamination.
	Buy prepared food Buy food that does not require much prepping or handling. For example, you could buy precooked chicken breasts or chopped lettuce.

Food handlers should avoid time-temperature abuse by following good policies and procedures. These should address the areas in Table 4.2.

Table 4.2: Avoiding Time-Temperature Abuse

Guideline	Description
	**Monitoring** Learn which food items should be checked, how often, and by whom. Make sure food handlers understand what to do, how to do it, and why it is important.
	Tools Make sure the correct kinds of thermometers are available. Give food handlers their own thermometers. Have them use timers in prep areas to check how long food is in the temperature danger zone.
	**Recording** Have food handlers record temperatures regularly. Make sure they write down when the temperatures were taken. Print simple forms for recording this information. Post them on clipboards outside of coolers and freezers, near prep areas, and next to cooking and holding equipment.
	Time and temperature control Have procedures to limit the time TCS food spends in the temperature danger zone. This might include limiting the amount of food that can be removed from a cooler when prepping the food.
	**Corrective actions** Make sure food handlers know what to do when time and temperature standards are not met. For example, if you hold soup on a steam table and its temperature falls below 135°F (57°C) after two hours, you might reheat it to the correct temperature or throw it out.

Something to Think About

A *Salmonella* outbreak linked to pastries claimed the lives of two people and sickened dozens of others. The bakery that made the pastries was cited for many violations during the investigation. One was for leaving a 5-gallon bucket of pastry cream to cool at room temperature. This kept the cream in the temperature danger zone for hours. Workers also stored ready-to-eat pastry shells in used egg crates. The egg crates later tested positive for *Salmonella*.

Apply Your Knowledge

An Ounce of Prevention   Write an X next to the practice if it helps prevent cross-contamination.

1. __X__   Use separate cutting boards for prepping raw meat and raw vegetables.

2. __X__   Wash and rinse a cutting board after prepping raw fish.

3. _____   Buy diced onions instead of dicing them in the operation.

4. _____   Prep salads before prepping raw meat on the same prep table.

5. __X__   Use green-handled knives to prep produce and yellow-handled knives to prep raw poultry.

6. __X__   Wipe down prep tables with a wiping cloth between different tasks.

7. _____   Cook chicken in-house instead of buying precooked chicken.

For answers, please turn to page 4.16.

145° Roasts of Beef Pork veal and and fish
155° Ground meat - Beef Pork Not poultry
165° Poultry and stuffed meat

Apply Your Knowledge

Is It Safe?   Read each story and decide if the food handler handled the food safely. Explain why or why not in the space provided.

1 Leah had to prepare six chicken salad sandwiches. She went to the cooler and pulled out a large hotel pan of chicken salad and put it on the prep table. She was interrupted several times to help with other tasks. After assembling the sandwiches, she covered the pan of chicken salad, dated it, and put it back in the cooler.

Did Leah handle the food safely? Why or why not?

_____

_____

_____

2 Greg filleted raw salmon on a cutting board on the prep table. Then he washed and rinsed the table and equipment he used. After that, he sliced onions and peppers on the same cutting board on the prep table. Before he left for the day, he washed, rinsed, and sanitized the prep table and equipment.

Did Greg handle the food safely? Why or why not?

_____

_____

_____

For answers, please turn to page 4.16.

Monitoring Time and Temperature

To keep food safe, you must control the amount of time it spends in the temperature danger zone. This requires monitoring. The most important tool you have to monitor temperature is the thermometer. Three types are commonly used in operations:

- Bimetallic stemmed thermometers
- Thermocouples
- Thermistors

Bimetallic Stemmed Thermometer

A bimetallic stemmed thermometer, shown in the photo at right, can check temperatures from 0°F to 220°F (–18°C to 104°C). This makes it useful for checking temperatures during the flow of food. For example, you can use it to check food temperatures during receiving. You can also use it to check food in a hot- or cold-holding unit.

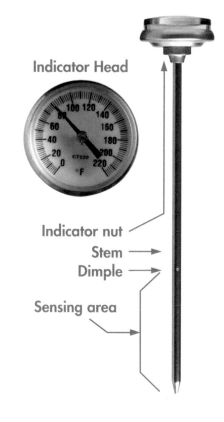

Indicator Head

Indicator nut

Stem →

Dimple →

Sensing area

A bimetallic stemmed thermometer measures temperature through its metal stem. When checking temperatures, insert the stem into the food up to the dimple. You must do this because the sensing area of the thermometer goes from the tip of the stem to the dimple. This trait makes this thermometer useful for checking the temperature of large or thick food. It is usually not practical for thin food, such as hamburger patties.

If you buy these thermometers for your operation, make sure they have these features.

Calibration nut   You can adjust the thermometer to make it accurate by using its calibration nut.

Easy-to-read markings   Clear markings reduce the chance that someone will misread the thermometer. The thermometer must be scaled in at least two-degree increments.

Dimple   The dimple is the mark on the stem that shows the end of the temperature-sensing area.

Thermocouples and Thermistors

Thermocouples, such as the one in the photo at right, and thermistors are also common types of thermometers in operations. These tools are similar. The difference between them is the technology inside.

Thermocouples and thermistors measure temperatures through a metal probe. Temperatures are displayed digitally. The sensing area on thermocouples and thermistors is on the tip of their probe. This means you do not have to insert them into the food as far as bimetallic stemmed thermometers to get a correct reading. Thermocouples and thermistors are good for checking the temperature of both thick and thin food.

Thermocouples and thermistors come in several styles and sizes. Many come with different types of probes. The following are some basic types.

Table 4.3: **Types of Probes**

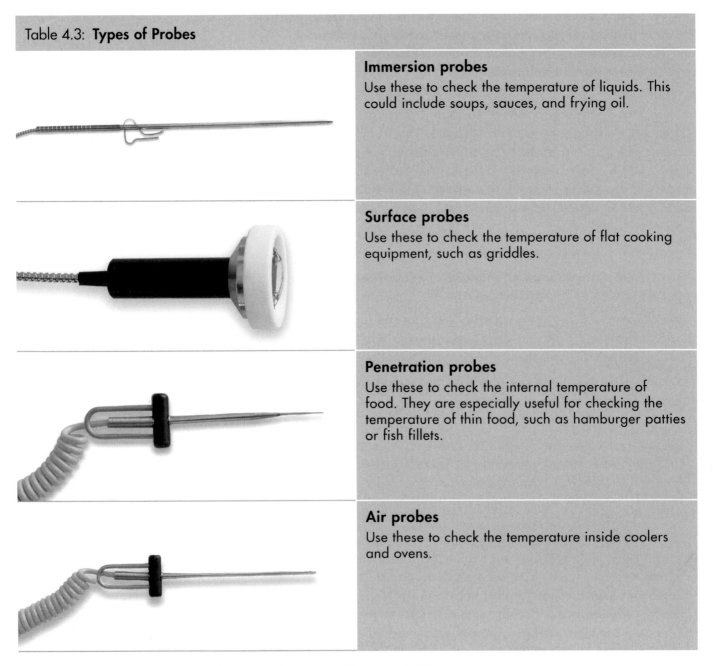

Immersion probes
Use these to check the temperature of liquids. This could include soups, sauces, and frying oil.

Surface probes
Use these to check the temperature of flat cooking equipment, such as griddles.

Penetration probes
Use these to check the internal temperature of food. They are especially useful for checking the temperature of thin food, such as hamburger patties or fish fillets.

Air probes
Use these to check the temperature inside coolers and ovens.

Infrared (Laser) Thermometers

Infrared thermometers measure the temperature of food and equipment surfaces. These thermometers are quick and easy to use.

Infrared thermometers do not need to touch a surface to check its temperature. This means there is less chance for cross-contamination and damage to food. However, these thermometers cannot measure air temperature or the internal temperature of food.

Follow these guidelines for using infrared thermometers.

Distance   Hold the thermometer as close to the food or equipment as you can without touching it as seen in the photo on the right.

Barriers   Remove anything between the thermometer and the food, food package, or equipment. Do **NOT** take readings through metal, such as stainless steel or aluminum. Do **NOT** take readings through glass.

Manufacturer's directions   Always follow the manufacturer's guidelines. This should give you the most accurate readings.

Other Temperature-Recording Devices

Other tools are available that can help you monitor temperature. A maximum registering thermometer is one type. This thermometer indicates the highest temperature reached during use and is used where temperature readings cannot be continuously observed. It works well for checking the final rinse temperature of dishwashing machines.

Some devices monitor both time and temperature. The time-temperature indicator (TTI) shown in the photo at right, is an example. These tags are attached to packaging by the supplier. A color change appears in the window if the food has been time-temperature abused during shipment or storage. This color change is not reversible, so you know if the food has been abused.

Some suppliers place temperature-recording devices inside their delivery trucks. These devices constantly check and record temperatures. You can check the device during receiving to make sure food was at safe temperatures while it was being shipped.

General Thermometer Guidelines

You should know how to use and care for each type of thermometer in your operation. In general, follow the guidelines below. However, you should always follow manufacturers' directions.

Cleaning and sanitizing   Thermometers must be washed, rinsed, sanitized (as seen in the photo at right), and air-dried. Keep storage cases clean, too. Do these things before and after using thermometers to prevent cross-contamination. Be sure the sanitizing solution you use is for food-contact surfaces. Always have plenty of clean and sanitized thermometers on hand.

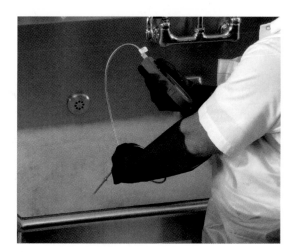

Calibration   Thermometers can lose their accuracy. When this happens, the thermometer must be calibrated, or adjusted, to give a correct reading. Make sure your thermometers are accurate by calibrating them regularly. Calibrate thermometers at these times:

- After they have been bumped or dropped.
- After they have been exposed to extreme temperature changes.
- Before deliveries arrive.
- Before each shift.

Keep in mind:

- Some thermometers cannot be calibrated and must be replaced.
- Others will need to be sent back to the manufacturer for calibration.
- Always follow the manufacturer's directions regarding calibration.

Accuracy   Thermometers used to measure the temperature of food must be accurate to within ±2°F or ±1°C. Thermometers used to measure air temperature in food-storage equipment must be accurate to within ±3°F or ±1.5°C. A hanging thermometer in a walk-in cooler is an example.

Glass thermometers   Glass thermometers, such as candy thermometers, can be a physical contaminant if they break. They can only be used when enclosed in a shatterproof casing.

Checking temperatures   When checking the temperature of food:

- Insert the probe into the thickest part of the food, as shown in the photo at left. This is usually in the center.
- Take another reading in a different spot. The temperature may vary in different areas.

Before recording a temperature, wait for the thermometer reading to steady. While digital thermometers are capable of displaying the temperature instantly, bimetallic stemmed thermometers will take more time. Allow at least 15 seconds after you insert the thermometer stem into the food.

Calibrating Thermometers

There are two ways to calibrate a thermometer:

- The boiling-point method involves adjusting the thermometer to the temperature at which water boils (212°F [100°C], depending on your elevation).

- The ice-point method involves adjusting the thermometer to the temperature at which water freezes (32°F [0°C]).

The ice-point method, detailed below, is easier and safer.

1 Fill a large container with ice. Use crushed ice if you have it. Add tap water until the container is full.

Note: Stir the mixture well.

2 Put the thermometer stem or probe into the ice water. Make sure the sensing area is submerged.

Wait 30 seconds or until the indicator stops moving.

Note: Do not let the stem or probe touch the container.

3 Adjust the thermometer so it reads 32°F (0°C).

Note: To calibrate a bimetallic stemmed thermometer, adjust it by holding the calibration nut with a wrench or other tool.

To calibrate a thermocouple or thermistor, follow the manufacturer's directions.

Apply Your Knowledge

Pick the Correct Thermometer   For each situation, choose the best thermometer or thermometers. Some thermometers may be chosen more than once. Write the letter or letters in the space provided.

1 _____ Internal temperature of a fish fillet

2 _____ Internal temperature of a roast

3 _____ Internal temperature of fryer oil

4 _____ Surface temperature of a griddle

5 _____ Air temperature of a cooler

A Bimetallic stemmed thermometer

B Thermocouple with immersion probe

C Thermocouple with surface probe

D Thermocouple with penetration probe

E Thermocouple with air probe

F Infrared thermometer

For answers, please turn to page 4.16.

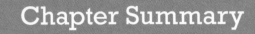

Chapter Summary

- The flow of food is the path food takes in your operation from purchasing to service. Many things can happen to food in its flow through the operation. Two major concerns are cross-contamination and time-temperature abuse.

- To prevent cross-contamination, keep ready-to-eat and raw food separated. When possible, use separate equipment for each type of food. Clean and sanitize all work surfaces, equipment, and utensils before and after each task. When separate equipment cannot be used, prep ready-to-eat food and raw meat, poultry, and fish at different times. Prepping ready-to-eat food first minimizes the chance for contamination. Similarly, you can buy food items that do not require much preparation or handling.

- Time-temperature abuse happens any time food remains between 41°F and 135°F (5°C and 57°C). This range is called the temperature danger zone. You must try to keep food out of this range.

- Have policies and procedures to avoid time-temperature abuse. They should include monitoring food and recording temperatures and times. Also make sure the correct types of thermometers are available. Use timers to check how long food is in the temperature danger zone. Make sure food handlers know what to do if time and temperature standards are not met.

- A thermometer is the most important tool you can use to prevent time-temperature abuse. Different types of thermometers are suited to different tasks. Use the correct type for the food or equipment being checked. Clean and sanitize thermometers before and after each use.

- When checking food temperatures, put the thermometer stem or probe into the thickest part of the food. Then take another reading in a different spot. Before you record the temperature, wait for the thermometer reading to steady. If using a bimetallic stemmed thermometer, put it into the food from the tip to the end of the sensing area. Never use glass thermometers with food items unless they are enclosed in a shatterproof casing.

- Thermometers should be calibrated regularly to keep them accurate. Two methods for calibrating are the ice-point method and the boiling-point method. Follow the manufacturer's directions for calibration.

Chapter Review Case Study

To keep food safe, you must prevent cross-contamination; prevent time-temperature abuse; check food temperatures using the correct kinds of thermometers; and keep your thermometers accurate.

Now, take what you have learned in this chapter and apply it to the following case study.

At 6:00 a.m., Annie started her workday at The Little Bistro. After a quick meeting with the chef, her first task was to make the broccoli quiches for the lunch special. By 6:15 a.m., she had collected all the ingredients. She set salt, eggs, cream, butter, and cheese on the prep table. On her last trip to the cooler, she got the broccoli. It took over an hour to wash and chop it. Finally, Annie was able to make the quiche filling. Leaving the leftover eggs and cream on the table, she got out the premade quiche crusts from the freezer and poured the filling. By the time she got the quiches in the oven, it was 10:45 a.m.

Twenty-five minutes later, Annie checked the quiches. They were supposed to bake for around 30 minutes. However, she did not want to overcook them. The chef said their internal temperature needed to be 155°F (68°C). Annie used an infrared thermometer to check the temperature of one quiche in two places. The readings were in the correct range. She took the quiches out of the oven and set them on a table to cool.

While the quiches cooled, Annie went to work making fruit salad. She washed her hands and put on gloves. As she headed back to the prep table with the melon, strawberries, and grapes, she noticed the eggs and cream she left out. She quickly put them back in the cooler. Then she wiped down the table and started prepping the melon.

What did Annie do wrong?

_____

_____

_____

_____

_____

_____

For answers, please turn to page 4.16.

Study Questions

Circle the best answer to each question.

1 **A food handler has finished trimming raw chicken on a cutting board and needs the board to prep vegetables. What must be done to the cutting board?**

A It must be dried with a paper towel.

B It must be turned over to the other side.

C It must be washed, rinsed, and sanitized.

D It must be rinsed in hot water and air-dried.

2 **How far must a bimetallic stemmed thermometer be inserted into food to give an accurate reading?**

A Just past the tip of the thermometer stem

B Halfway between the tip of the thermometer stem and the dimple

C To the dimple in the thermometer stem

D Past the dimple of the thermometer stem

3 **Which probe should be used to check the temperature of a chicken breast?**

A Air probe

B Immersion probe

C Penetration probe

D Surface probe

4 **At what temperatures do most foodborne pathogens grow most quickly?**

A Between 0°F and 41°F (-17°C and 5°C)

B Between 45°F and 65°F (7°C and 18°C)

C Between 70°F and 125°F (21°C and 52°C)

D Between 130°F and 165°F (54°C and 74°C)

5 **Which practice can help prevent time-temperature abuse?**

A Keeping records of employee schedules

B Cleaning and sanitizing equipment and work surfaces

C Making sure food handlers spend at least 30 seconds washing their hands

D Limiting the amount of food that can be removed from a cooler for prepping

Study Questions

6 **Which thermometer is used to measure surface temperatures?**

A   Thermistor

B   Thermocouple

C   Infrared thermometer

D   Bimetallic stemmed thermometer

7 **A thermometer used to measure the temperature of food must be accurate to what temperature?**

A   ±2°F or ±1°C

B   ±4°F or ±3°C

C   ±6°F or ±5°C

D   ±8°F or ±7°C

8 **Which practice can help prevent cross-contamination?**

A   Using color-coded cutting boards

B   Rinsing cutting boards between use

C   Purchasing food requiring preparation

D   Prepping raw and ready-to-eat food at the same time

9 **What device can be used to monitor both time and temperature abuse during the shipment or storage of food?**

A   Infrared thermometer

B   Time-temperature indicator

C   Thermistor with an air probe

D   Bimetallic stemmed thermometer

10 **How long can food stay in the temperature danger zone before it must be thrown out?**

A   1 hour

B   2 hours

C   3 hours

D   4 hours

For answers, please turn to page 4.17.

Answers

4.5 An Ounce of Prevention

1, 3, 4, and 5 should be marked.

4.6 Is It Safe?

1 No. Leah took out more chicken salad than she needed to make a small number of sandwiches. This exposed the chicken salad to time-temperature abuse, which was made worse by the many interruptions.

2 No. Greg did not sanitize the table and equipment after he filleted the salmon. The onions and peppers could have been contaminated by the salmon.

4.11 Pick the Correct Thermometer

1 A, D

2 A, D

3 B

4 C, F

5 E

4.13 Chapter Review Case Study

Annie did the following things wrong:

- She should have washed her hands before making the quiches.

- She left the eggs and dairy at room temperature for too long. The quiche filling was at room temperature for four hours and 30 minutes. The leftover eggs and dairy were at room temperature for five hours. She should have thrown away the leftover eggs and dairy.

- She used the wrong kind of thermometer to check the internal temperature of the quiches.

- She let the quiches cool at room temperature and did not store them correctly.

- She did not clean and sanitize the prep table after she finished preparing the quiches and before prepping the fruit.

Answers

4.14   Study Questions

1 C
2 C
3 C
4 C
5 D
6 C
7 A
8 A
9 B
10 D

General Purchasing and Receiving Principles

You cannot make unsafe food safe. So, you must make sure you only bring safe food into your operation. Purchasing food from approved, reputable suppliers and following good receiving procedures will help to ensure the safety and quality of the food your operation uses.

Something to Think About

An elderly woman died and nearly 300 people were sickened with Hepatitis A after eating at two of a franchise restaurant's 11 locations. The source of the outbreak was identified as frozen scallops, which were eaten raw. The two stores purchased the tainted scallops from the same supplier.

Purchasing

Before you accept any deliveries, you must make sure that the food you purchase is safe. Follow these guidelines.

Approved, reputable suppliers   Food must be purchased from approved, reputable suppliers. These suppliers have been inspected and can show you an inspection report. They also meet all applicable local, state, and federal laws. This applies to all suppliers in the supply chain. Your operation's chain can include growers, shippers, packers, manufacturers, distributors (trucking fleets and warehouses), and local markets.

Develop a relationship with your suppliers, and get to know their food safety practices. In the photo at left, an owner is meeting with a supplier and touring the facility. Consider reviewing suppliers' most recent inspection reports. These reports can be from the U.S. Department of Agriculture (USDA), the Food and Drug Administration (FDA), or a third-party inspector. They should be based on Good Manufacturing Practices (GMP) or Good Agricultural Practices (GAP).

Make sure the inspection report reviews the following areas:

- Receiving and storage
- Processing
- Shipping
- Cleaning and sanitizing
- Personal hygiene
- Staff training
- Recall program
- HACCP program or other food safety system

Many operations establish supplier lists based on their company specifications, standards, and procedures. However, only approved suppliers should be included on these lists.

Deliveries   Suppliers must deliver food when staff has enough time to do inspections. Schedule deliveries at a time when they can be correctly received.

Receiving and Inspecting

You must take action to ensure that the receiving and inspection process is smooth and safe:

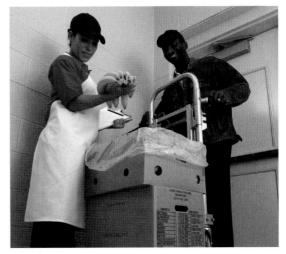

- Make specific staff responsible for receiving. Train them to follow food safety guidelines. In the photo at right, a food handler is inspecting produce.

- Provide staff with the tools they need, including purchase orders, thermometers, and scales.

- Make sure enough trained staff are available to receive and inspect food items promptly. Deliveries must be inspected immediately upon receipt.

The process starts with a visual inspection of the delivery truck. Check it for signs of contamination. Inspect the overall condition of the vehicle. Look for signs of pests. If there are of signs of problems, reject the delivery.

Continue with a visual inspection of food items. Make sure they have been received at the correct temperature. Once inspected, food items must be stored as quickly as possible in the correct areas. This is especially true for refrigerated and frozen items.

Key Drop Deliveries

Some foodservice operations receive food after-hours when they are closed for business. This is often referred to as a key drop delivery. The supplier is given a key or other access to the operation to make the delivery. Products are then placed in coolers, freezers, and dry-storage areas. The delivery must be inspected once you arrive at the operation and must meet the following conditions:

- It is from an approved source.
- It was placed in the correct storage location to maintain the required temperature.
- It was protected from contamination in storage.
- It has not been contaminated.
- It is honestly presented.

Rejecting Items

If you must reject an item, set it aside from the items you are accepting. Then tell the delivery person exactly what is wrong with the rejected item. Make sure you get a signed adjustment or credit slip before giving the item back to the delivery person. Finally, log the incident on the invoice or the receiving document.

Occasionally, you may be able to recondition and use items that would have been rejected. For example, a shipment of cans with contaminated surfaces may be cleaned and sanitized, allowing them to be used. However, the same cans may not be reconditioned if they are damaged.

Recalls

Food items you have received may sometimes be recalled by the manufacturer. This may happen when food contamination is confirmed or suspected. It can also occur when items have been mislabeled or misbranded. Often food is recalled when food allergens have not been identified on the label. Most vendors will notify you of the recall. However, you should also monitor recall notifications made by the FDA and the USDA.

Follow these guidelines when notified of a recall:

- Identify the recalled food items by matching information from the recall notice to the item. This may include the manufacturer's ID, the time the item was manufactured, and the item's use-by date.

- Remove the item from inventory, and place it in a secure and appropriate location. That may be a cooler or dry-storage area. The recalled item must be stored separately from food, utensils, equipment, linens, and single-use items.

- Label the item in a way that will prevent it from being placed back in inventory. Some operations do this by including a "Do Not Use" and "Do Not Discard" label on recalled food items, as shown in the photo at right. Inform staff not to use the product.

- Refer to the vendor's notification or recall notice for what to do with the item. For example, you might be instructed to throw it out or return it to the vendor.

Temperature

Use thermometers to check food temperatures during receiving.

Checking the Temperature of Various Types of Food   The following examples explain how to check the temperatures of various types of food.

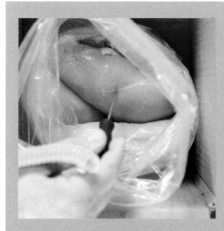  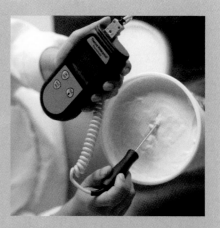

Meat, poultry, and fish

Insert the thermometer stem or probe directly into the thickest part of the food. The center is usually the thickest part.

Reduced-oxygen packaging (ROP) food (modified atmosphere packaging [MAP], vacuum-packed, and sous vide food)

Insert the thermometer stem or probe between two packages. If the package allows, fold it around the thermometer stem or probe. Be careful **NOT** to puncture the package.

Other packaged food

Open the package and insert the thermometer stem or probe into the food. The sensing area must be fully immersed in the food. The stem or probe must **NOT** touch the package.

Delivery temperatures   Deliveries should also meet the temperature criteria in Table 5.1.

Table 5.1: **Temperatures for Food Deliveries**

Food	Receiving Criteria
	Cold TCS food Receive at 41°F (5°C) or lower, unless otherwise specified.
	Live shellfish (oysters, mussels, clams, and scallops) • Receive at an air temperature of 45°F (7°C) and an internal temperature no greater than 50°F (10°C). • Cool the shellfish to 41°F (5°C) or lower in four hours.
	Shucked shellfish • Receive at 45°F (7°C) or lower. • Cool the shellfish to 41°F (5°C) or lower in four hours.
	Milk • Receive at 45°F (7°C) or lower. • Cool the milk to 41°F (5°C) or lower in four hours.
	Shell eggs Receive at an air temperature of 45°F (7°C) or lower.
	Hot TCS food Receive at 135°F (57°C) or higher.
	Frozen food Frozen food should be frozen solid when received. **REJECT** frozen food for the following reasons. • Fluids or water stains appear in case bottoms or on packaging. • There are ice crystals or frozen liquids on the food or the packaging. This may be evidence of thawing and refreezing, which shows the food has been time-temperature abused.

Packaging

Both food items and nonfood items such as single-use cups, utensils, and napkins must be packaged correctly when you receive them. Items should be delivered in their original packaging with a manufacturer's label. The packaging should be intact and clean. It also should protect food and food-contact surfaces from contamination. Reject food and nonfood items if packaging has any of the following problems.

Damage   Reject items with tears, holes, or punctures in their packaging. Likewise, reject cans if they have any of these problems:

* Severe dents in the can seams, as shown at right
* Deep dents in the can body
* Missing labels
* Swollen or bulging ends
* Holes and visible signs of leaking
* Rust

All food packaged in a reduced-oxygen environment, such as vacuum-packed meat, must be rejected if the packaging is bloated or leaking. Items with broken cartons or seals or with dirty and discolored packaging should also be rejected. Do **NOT** accept cases or packages that appear to have been tampered with.

Liquid   Reject items with leaks, dampness, or water stains (which indicate the item was wet at some point), as shown in the photo at right.

Pests   Reject items with signs of pests or pest damage.

Dates   Food items must be correctly labeled. Do **NOT** accept food that is missing a use-by date or expiration date from the manufacturer. This date is the recommended last date for the product to be at peak quality. Reject items that have passed their use-by or expiration dates. Some operations label food items with the date the item was received to help with stock rotation during storage.

You may see other dates on labels. A sell-by date tells the store how long to display the product for sale. A best-by date is the date by which the product should be eaten for best flavor or quality.

Documents

Food items must be delivered with the correct documents. For example, shellfish must be received with a shellstock identification tag. These tags indicate when and where the shellfish were harvested. They also ensure that the shellfish are from an approved source.

Store shellfish in their original container. Do **NOT** remove the shellstock tag from the container until the last shellfish has been used. When the last shellfish is removed from the container, write the date on the shellstock tag. Then, keep the tag on file for 90 days from that date.

Fish that will be eaten raw or partially cooked must also be received with the correct documentation. These documents must indicate the fish was correctly frozen before you received it. Keep these documents for 90 days from the sale of the fish. If the fish was farm raised, it must have documentation that states the fish was raised to FDA standards. These documents must also be kept for 90 days from the sale of the fish.

Food Quality

Poor food quality can be a sign that the food has been time-temperature abused and, therefore, may be unsafe. Work with your suppliers to define specific safety and quality criteria for the food items you typically receive. Reject food if it has any of the following problems.

Appearance   Reject food that is moldy or has an abnormal color, as shown in the photo at left. Food that is moist when it should be dry, such as salami, should also be rejected. Do **NOT** accept any food item that shows signs of pests or pest damage.

Texture   Reject meat, fish, or poultry that is slimy, sticky, or dry. Also reject it if it has soft flesh that leaves an imprint when you touch it.

Odor   Reject food with an abnormal or unpleasant odor.

In addition to the guidelines above, you should always reject any item that does not meet your company's standards for quality.

Apply Your Knowledge

Accept or Reject?   Write an A next to the food items you should accept. Write an R next to the food items you should reject.

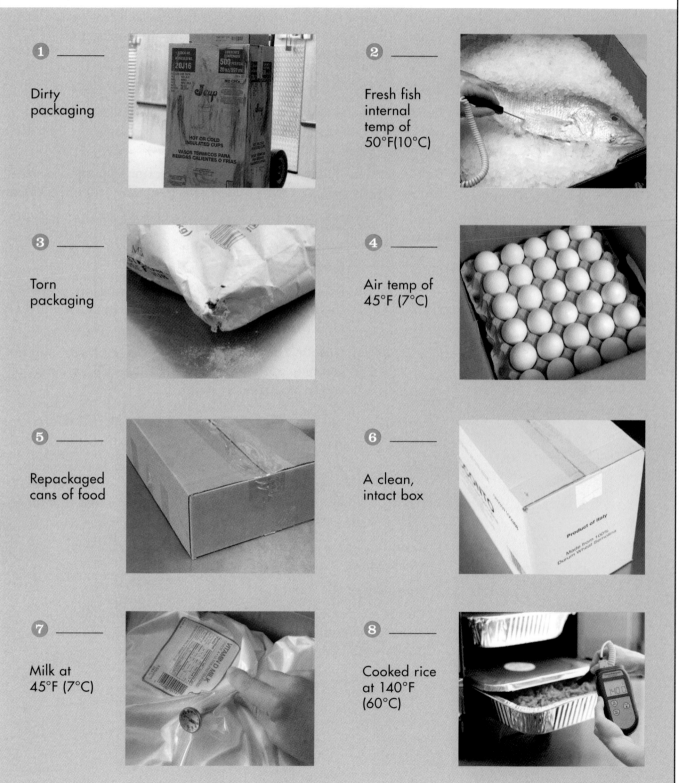

1 _____

Dirty packaging

2 _____

Fresh fish internal temp of 50°F(10°C)

3 _____

Torn packaging

4 _____

Air temp of 45°F (7°C)

5 _____

Repackaged cans of food

6 _____

A clean, intact box

7 _____

Milk at 45°F (7°C)

8 _____

Cooked rice at 140°F (60°C)

For answers, please turn to page 5.22.

Storing

Following good storage guidelines for food and nonfood items will help keep these items safe and preserve their quality. In general, you must label and date mark your food correctly. You must also rotate food and store it at the correct temperature. Finally, you need to store items in a way that prevents cross-contamination.

Labeling

Labeling food is important for many reasons. Illnesses have occurred when unlabeled chemicals were mistaken for food such as flour, sugar, and baking powder.

Customers have also suffered allergic reactions when food was unknowingly prepped with a food allergen that was not labeled.

Labeling Food for Use On-site

- All items that are not in their original containers must be labeled.

- Food labels should include the common name of the food or a statement that clearly and accurately identifies it, as shown in the photo at left.

- It is not necessary to label food if it clearly will not be mistaken for another item. The food must be easily identified by sight.

Labeling Food That Is Packaged On-site for Retail Sale

Food packaged in the operation that is being sold to customers for use at home, such as bottled salad dressing, must be labeled. The label must include the following information:

- Common name of the food or a statement that clearly identifies it.

- Quantity of the food.

- List of ingredients and subingredients in descending order by weight. This is necessary if the item contains two or more ingredients.

- List of artificial colors and flavors in the food.
- Chemical preservatives.
- Name and place of business of the manufacturer, packer, or distributor.
- Source of each major food allergen contained in the food. This is not necessary if the source is already part of the common name of the ingredient.

These labeling requirements do not apply to customers' leftover food items placed in carry-out containers.

Date Marking

Refrigeration slows the growth of most bacteria, but some types grow well at refrigeration temperatures. When food is refrigerated for long periods of time, these bacteria can grow enough to cause illness. For this reason, ready-to-eat TCS food must be marked if held for longer than 24 hours. The label must indicate when the food must be sold, eaten, or thrown out, as shown in the photo at right.

Ready-to-eat TCS food can be stored for only seven days if it is held at 41°F (5°C) or lower. After that date, the food must be discarded. The count begins on the day that the food was prepared or a commercial container was opened. For example, a food handler who prepared and stored potato salad on October 1 would write a discard date of October 7 on the label.

Operations have a variety of systems for date marking. Some write the day or date the food was prepped on the label. Others write the use-by day or date on the label.

Sometimes, commercially processed food will have a use-by date that is less than seven days from the date the container was opened. In this case, the container should be marked with this use-by date, as long as the date is based on food safety.

When combining food with different use-by dates in a dish, the discard date of the dish should be based on the earliest use-by date of any food items involved. Here is an example:

- A food handler is prepping a jambalaya on December 4 using shrimp and sausage.

- The shrimp has a use-by date of December 8.

- The sausage has a use-by date of December 10.

- So, the use-by date of the jambalaya is December 8.

December						
Sunday	Monday	Tuesday	Wednesday	Thursday	Friday	Saturday
				1	2	3
4 Jambalaya Prep Date	5	6	7	8 Shrimp Use-By Jambalaya Use-By	9	10 Sausage Use-By
11	12	13	14	15	16	17

Temperatures

Pathogens can grow when food is not stored at the correct temperature. Follow these guidelines to keep food safe:

- Store TCS food at an internal temperature of 41°F (5°C) or lower or 135°F (57°C) or higher.

- Store frozen food at temperatures that keep it frozen.

- Make sure storage units have at least one air temperature measuring device. It must be accurate to +/- 3°F or +/- 1.5°C. This device must be located in the warmest part of refrigerated units and the coldest part of hot-holding units. The hanging thermometer in the photo at left is a common type of temperature measuring device used in coolers.

- Do not overload coolers or freezers. Storing too many food items prevents good airflow and makes the units work harder to stay cold. Be aware that frequent opening of the cooler lets warm air inside, which can affect food safety.

- Use open shelving. Do **NOT** line shelves with aluminum foil, sheet pans, or paper. This restricts the circulation of cold air in the unit.

- Monitor food temperatures regularly. Randomly sample the temperature of stored food to verify that the cooler is working. If the food is not at the correct temperature, throw it out.

Rotation

Food must be rotated in storage to maintain quality and limit the growth of pathogens. Food items must be rotated so that those with the earliest use-by or expiration dates are used before items with later dates.

Many operations use the first-in, first-out (FIFO) method to rotate their refrigerated, frozen, and dry food during storage. Here is one way to use the FIFO method:

1 Identify the food item's use-by or expiration date.

2 Store items with the earliest use-by or expiration dates in front of items with later dates, as shown in the photo at right.

3 Once items are shelved, use those items stored in front first.

4 Throw out food that has passed its manufacturer's use-by or expiration date.

Preventing Cross-Contamination

Food must be stored in ways that prevent cross-contamination. Follow the guidelines throughout this section.

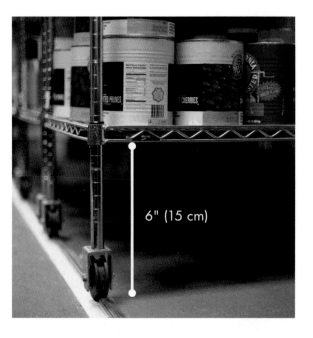

6" (15 cm)

Supplies

- Store all items in designated storage areas.

- Store items away from walls and at least six inches (15 centimeters) off the floor, as shown in the photo at left.

- Store single-use items (e.g., sleeve of single-use cups, single-use gloves) in original packaging.

Containers

- Store food in containers intended for food.

- Use containers that are durable, leakproof, and able to be sealed or covered.

- **NEVER** use empty food containers to store chemicals. **NEVER** put food in empty chemical containers.

Cleaning

Keep all storage areas clean and dry. Clean floors, walls, and shelving in coolers, freezers, dry-storage areas, and heated holding cabinets on a regular basis. Clean up spills and leaks promptly to keep them from contaminating other food. Also follow these guidelines:

- Clean dollies, carts, transporters, and trays often.

- Store food in containers that have been cleaned and sanitized.

- Store dirty linens away from food. Store them in clean, nonabsorbent containers. They can also be stored in washable laundry bags.

Storage Order

Safe food storage starts with wrapping or covering food. After that, how you store the food depends on the type of food and your options for storage.

- Store raw meat, poultry, and seafood separately from ready-to-eat food. If raw and ready-to-eat food cannot be stored separately, store ready-to-eat food above raw meat, poultry, and seafood, as shown on the following page. This will prevent juices from raw food from dripping onto ready-to-eat food.

- Raw meat, poultry, and seafood can be stored with or above ready-to-eat food in a freezer if all of the items have been commercially processed and packaged. Frozen food that is being thawed in coolers must also be stored below ready-to-eat food.

- Store raw meat, poultry, and seafood in coolers in the following top-to-bottom order, as shown below: seafood, whole cuts of beef and pork, ground meat and ground fish, whole and ground poultry. This order is based on the minimum internal cooking temperature of each food.

- As an exception, ground meat and ground fish can be stored above whole cuts of beef and pork. To do this, make sure the packaging keeps out pathogens and chemicals. It also must not leak.

Storage Order, Top to Bottom	Minimum Internal Cooking Temperature
A Ready-to-eat food	N/A
B Seafood	145°F (63°C)
C Whole cuts of beef and pork	145°F (63°C)
D Ground meat and ground fish	155°F (68°C)
E Whole and ground poultry	165°F (74°C)

Storage Location

Food should be stored in a clean, dry location away from dust and other contaminants. To prevent contamination, NEVER store food in these areas:

- Locker rooms or dressing rooms
- Restrooms or garbage rooms
- Mechanical rooms
- Under unshielded sewer lines or leaking water lines
- Under stairwells

Damaged, Spoiled, or Incorrectly Stored Food

If you find expired, damaged, spoiled, or incorrectly stored food that has become unsafe, you should discard it. This includes food that is missing a date mark, ready-to-eat TCS food that has exceeded its date mark, and food that has exceeded time/temperature requirements.

If the food must be stored until it can be returned to the vendor, there is a risk of contaminating the food stored near it. To prevent this risk, follow these guidelines:

- Store the food away from other food and equipment.
- Label the food so food handlers do not use the product. The photo at left shows food that is properly labeled and stored until it can be returned to the vendor.

Apply Your Knowledge

What's Wrong with This Picture?   Find and circle the unsafe storage practices in this picture.

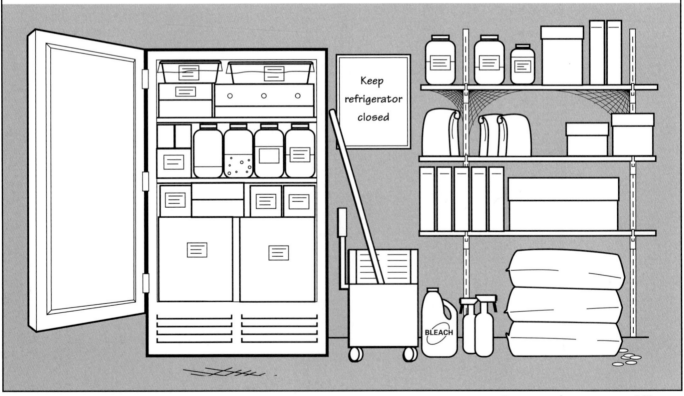

For answers, please turn to page 5.22.

Apply Your Knowledge

Load the Cooler   Next to the number of each food item, write the letter of the shelf it belongs on.

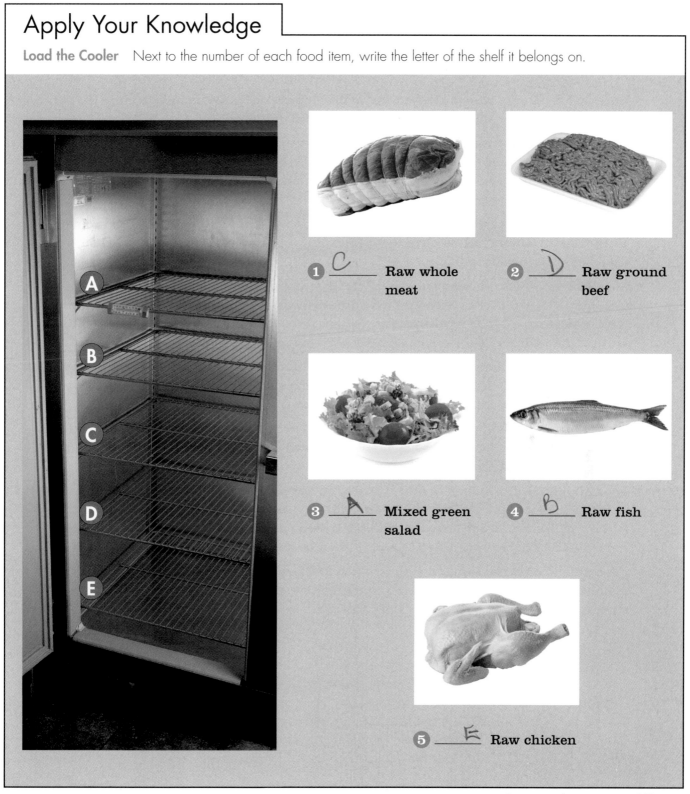

1 _C_ **Raw whole meat**

2 _D_ **Raw ground beef**

3 _A_ **Mixed green salad**

4 _B_ **Raw fish**

5 _E_ **Raw chicken**

For answers, please turn to page 5.22.

Chapter Summary

- Purchase food only from approved, reputable suppliers. These suppliers must be inspected and meet applicable local, state, and federal laws.

- Deliveries must be immediately inspected by designated staff. The staff must be trained to follow food safety guidelines and have the proper tools. The inspections include a visual check of the food and checks to make sure the food was received at the correct temperature.

- Sometimes food items are recalled by the manufacturer. Identify these items, remove them from inventory, and secure them in an appropriate location. Mark them so that staff does not use them.

- Cold TCS food must be received at 41°F (5°C) or lower. Hot TCS food must be received at 135°F (57°C) or higher. Frozen food should always be received frozen. Some items have other temperature requirements. Received food should have the correct color, texture, and odor.

- The packaging of delivered food items must be intact and clean, and it must protect food from contamination. There should also be no signs of pests or dampness. Food items should be correctly labeled and contain the correct documentation.

- Food must be stored in ways that prevent cross-contamination. Raw meat, poultry, and seafood should be stored separately from ready-to-eat food. If this is not possible, store ready-to-eat food above raw meat, poultry, and seafood.

- Food should be labeled before it is stored. The label should include the common name of the food. If TCS food was prepped in-house and will be stored longer than 24 hours, it must also be date marked. This food can be stored for only seven days if held at 41°F (5°C) or lower. After that, it must be discarded.

- Food should only be stored in a designated storage area. It should be stored away from walls and at least six inches (15 centimeters) off the floor. Stored food items should always be rotated so that older items are used first.

Chapter Review Case Study

To keep food safe during purchasing, receiving, and storage, you must know how to purchase food from approved, reputable suppliers; use criteria to accept and reject food during receiving; label and date food; and store food and nonfood items to prevent time-temperature abuse and contamination.

Now, take what you have learned in this chapter and apply it to the following case study.

A shipment was delivered to Francesca's Italian Restaurant on a warm summer day. Alyce, who was in charge of receiving, began inspecting the shipment. First, she inspected the bags of frozen shrimp. Alyce noticed the ice crystals inside the bags and took that as a good sign that the shrimp were still frozen.

Next, she used a thermometer to test the temperature of the vacuum-packed packages of ground beef, which was 40°F (4°C). Then Alyce used the same thermometer to measure the temperature of the fresh salmon. The salmon was on ice, although it seemed as though much of the ice had melted. The internal temperature of the salmon was 43°F (6°C), and the flesh sprung back after she touched it. She accepted the ground beef and the salmon.

Once she finished receiving the food, Alyce was ready to put it into storage. First, she carried the bags of shrimp to the freezer. Next, she wheeled several cases of fresh ground beef and the fresh salmon over to the walk-in cooler. She noticed that the readout on the outside of the cooler indicated 39°F (4°C). Alyce pushed through the cold curtains and bumped into a stockpot of soup as she moved inside. She moved the soup over and made a space for the ground beef. She was able to put the salmon on the shelf above the soup.

1 What receiving and storage mistakes did Alyce make?

_____

_____

_____

_____

_____

_____

For answers, please turn to page 5.23.

Study Questions

Circle the best answer to each question.

1 **What is the most important factor in choosing a food supplier?**

   A   It is recommended by others in the industry.

   B   It has a HACCP program or other food safety system.

   C   It has documented manufacturing and packing practices.

   D   It has been inspected and complies with local, state, and federal laws.

2 **What is the best method of checking the temperature of vacuum-packed meat?**

   A   Lay the thermometer stem or probe on the surface of the top package.

   B   Place the thermometer stem or probe between two packages of product.

   C   Open a package and insert the thermometer stem or probe into the product.

   D   Insert the thermometer stem or probe through the package into the product.

3 **What is the correct temperature for receiving cold TCS food?**

   A   32°F (0°C) or lower

   B   41°F (5°C) or lower

   C   45°F (7°C) or lower

   D   50°F (10°C) or lower

4 **Milk can be received at 45°F (7°C) under what condition?**

   A   It is thrown out after 2 days.

   B   It is cooled to 41°F (5°C) or lower in 4 hours.

   C   It is immediately cooled to 41°F (5°C) or lower.

   D   It is served or used in the operation within 2 hours.

5 **What causes large ice crystals to form on frozen food and its packaging?**

   A   Cross-contact

   B   Cross-contamination

   C   Time-temperature abuse

   D   Incorrect cleaning and sanitizing

Study Questions

6 Whole potatoes were coated with olive oil and salt, baked in-house, and stored in a cooler for several days. What must be included on the label for the baked potatoes?

A List of all ingredients

B List of common allergens

C Date that the food was received

D Date that the food should be discarded

7 When must you discard tuna salad that was prepped on July 19?

A July 21

B July 23

C July 25

D July 27

8 What is the problem with storing raw ground turkey above raw ground pork?

A Cross-contamination

B Poor personal hygiene

C Time-temperature abuse

D Cross-contact with allergens

9 Due to an operation's space limits, ready-to-eat and uncooked foods must be stored in the same cooler. How should foods be stored, in top-to-bottom order?

A According to the FIFO method, with oldest items on the top shelf and the newest items on the bottom

B According to preparation dates, with the earliest dates on the top shelf and the latest dates on the bottom

C According to minimum internal cooking temperatures, with ready-to-eat foods on the top shelf and poultry on the bottom

D According to minimum acceptable storage temperatures, with foods that can tolerate the warmest temperature on the top shelf and foods needing the coldest temperature on the bottom

10 How many inches (centimeters) from the floor should food be stored?

A At least 1 inch (3 cm)

B At least 2 inches (5 cm)

C At least 4 inches (10 cm)

D At least 6 inches (15 cm)

For answers, please turn to page 5.23.

Answers

5.9 Accept or Reject?

1 R

2 R

3 R

4 A

5 R

6 A

7 A

8 A

5.16 What's Wrong with This Picture?

Here are the unsafe storage practices:

- Chemicals stored with food
- Food stored on the floor
- Boxes of food not labeled
- Spilled food not cleaned up
- Cooler door open
- Overstocked cooler
- Area not clean
- Unlabeled items in cooler

5.17 Load the Cooler

1 C

2 D

3 A

4 B

5 E

Answers

5.19 Chapter Review Case Study

Alyce made the following receiving and storage mistakes:

* She should have rejected the shrimp. The ice crystals are evidence of thawing and refreezing.

* She did not clean and sanitize the probe she had used to measure the temperature of the ground beef and the fish.

* She should have rejected the salmon. The temperature of the fish was above 41°F (5°C), and the melted ice could be evidence of time-temperature abuse.

* Alyce checked the cooler's readout temperature, which was good, but she also should have spot-checked the internal temperatures of the food stored inside.

* Alyce put the raw salmon above ready-to-eat food (soup).

5.20 Study Questions

1 D

2 B

3 B

4 B

5 C

6 D

7 C

8 A

9 C

10 D

Preparation

Cross-contamination and time-temperature abuse can happen easily when you are preparing food. But, you can prevent pathogens from spreading and growing by making good food-prep choices.

General Preparation Practices

No matter what type of food you are prepping, you should begin by following these guidelines:

Equipment   Make sure workstations, cutting boards, and utensils are clean and sanitized.

Quantity   Only remove as much food from the cooler as you can prep in a short period of time. This keeps ingredients from sitting out for long periods of time. In the photo at left, the food handler has taken out too much tuna salad.

Storage   Return prepped food to the cooler, or cook it, as quickly as possible.

Additives   If you use food or color additives when prepping food, follow these guidelines:

* Only use additives that have been approved by your local regulatory authority. **NEVER** use more than is allowed by law. **NEVER** use additives to alter the appearance of the food.

* Do **NOT** sell produce that was treated with sulfites before it was received in the operation. **NEVER** add sulfites to produce that will be eaten raw.

Presentation Food must be offered to customers in a way that does not mislead or misinform them. Customers must be able to judge the true appearance, color, and quality of food. Do **NOT** use the following to misrepresent the appearance of food:

- Food additives or color additives
- Colored overwraps
- Lights

Food also must be presented the way it was described. For example, if your menu offers "Fried Perch," you cannot substitute another fish for the perch.

Food that has not been honestly presented must be thrown out.

Corrective actions Food that has become unsafe must be thrown out unless it can be safely reconditioned. All food—especially ready-to-eat food—must be thrown out in the following situations:

- When it is handled by staff who have been restricted or excluded from the operation due to illness
- When it is contaminated by hands or bodily fluids, for example, from sneezing
- When it has exceeded the time and temperature requirements designed to keep food safe

Sometimes food can be restored to a safe condition. This is called reconditioning. For example, a hot food that has not been held at the correct temperature may be reheated if it has not been in the temperature danger zone for more than two hours. This can return food to a safe condition.

Thawing

When frozen food is thawed and exposed to the temperature danger zone, pathogens in the food will begin to grow. To reduce this growth, **NEVER** thaw food at room temperature.

General Guidelines for TCS Food

Thaw TCS food according to the methods and guidelines in Table 6.1.

Table 6.1: Methods and Guidelines for Thawing TCS Food

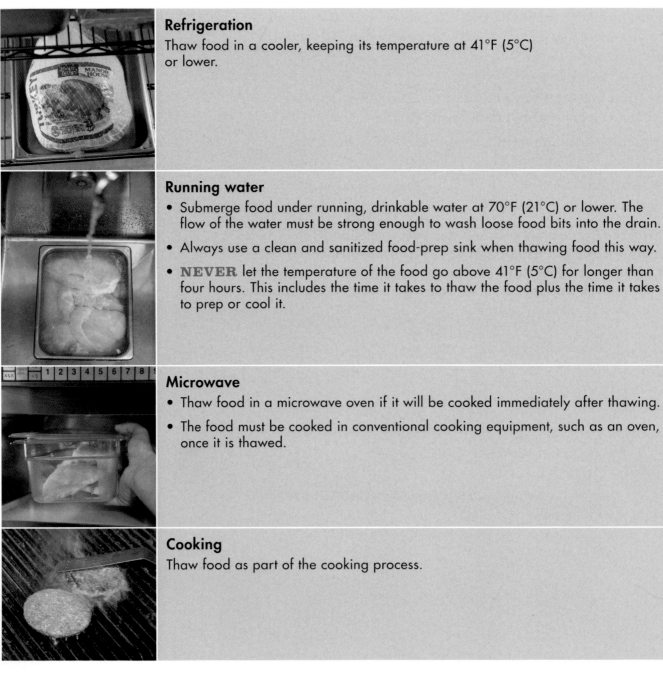

Method	Guidelines
Refrigeration	Thaw food in a cooler, keeping its temperature at 41°F (5°C) or lower.
Running water	• Submerge food under running, drinkable water at 70°F (21°C) or lower. The flow of the water must be strong enough to wash loose food bits into the drain. • Always use a clean and sanitized food-prep sink when thawing food this way. • **NEVER** let the temperature of the food go above 41°F (5°C) for longer than four hours. This includes the time it takes to thaw the food plus the time it takes to prep or cool it.
Microwave	• Thaw food in a microwave oven if it will be cooked immediately after thawing. • The food must be cooked in conventional cooking equipment, such as an oven, once it is thawed.
Cooking	Thaw food as part of the cooking process.

Thawing ROP Fish

Frozen fish may be supplied in reduced-oxygen packaging (ROP). This fish should usually remain frozen until ready for use. If this is stated on the label, the fish must be removed from the packaging at the following times:

- Before thawing it under refrigeration

- Before or immediately after thawing it under running water

Prepping Specific Food

Special care must be taken when handling ice and when preparing produce, eggs, and salads that contain TCS food.

Produce

When prepping produce, follow these guidelines:

Cross-contamination   **Make sure fruit and vegetables do NOT** touch surfaces exposed to raw meat, seafood, or poultry.

Washing   **Wash produce thoroughly under running water.** This is especially important before cutting it, cooking it, or combining it with other ingredients.

- The water should be a little warmer than the produce.

- Pay special attention to leafy greens such as lettuce and spinach, as the food handler in the photo at right is doing. Remove the outer leaves. Pull the lettuce or spinach completely apart and rinse thoroughly.

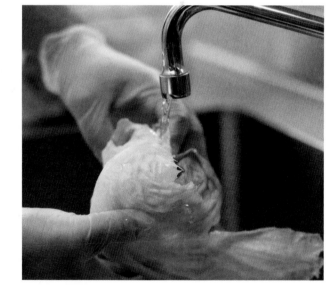

- Certain chemicals may be used to wash fruits and vegetables. Also, produce can be treated by washing it in water containing ozone. This treatment helps control pathogens. Your local regulatory authority can tell what is acceptable to use for this.

Soaking or storing   **When soaking or storing** produce in standing water or an ice-water slurry, do **NOT** mix different items or multiple batches of the same item.

Fresh-cut produce   **Refrigerate and hold sliced melons,** cut tomatoes, and cut leafy greens at 41°F (5°C) or lower. Many operations hold other fresh-cut produce at this temperature as well.

Raw seed sprouts   **If your operation primarily serves high-** risk populations, do **NOT** serve raw seed sprouts.

Eggs and Egg Mixtures

When prepping eggs and egg mixtures, follow these guidelines:

Pooled eggs   Handle pooled eggs (if allowed by your local regulatory authority) carefully. Pooled eggs are eggs that are cracked open and combined in a container, as shown in the photo at left. Cook them promptly after mixing, or store them at 41°F (5°C) or lower. Clean and sanitize the containers used to hold them before making a new batch.

Pasteurized eggs   Consider using pasteurized shell eggs or egg products when prepping egg dishes that need little or no cooking. Examples include Caesar salad dressing, hollandaise sauce, tiramisu, and mousse.

High-risk populations   If you mainly serve high-risk populations, such as those in hospitals and nursing homes, use pasteurized eggs or egg products when serving dishes that are raw or undercooked. Shell eggs that are pooled must also be pasteurized. You may use unpasteurized shell eggs if the dish will be cooked all the way through, such as with an omelet or a cake.

Salads Containing TCS Food

Chicken, tuna, egg, pasta, and potato salads have all been involved in foodborne-illness outbreaks. These salads are not usually cooked after preparation. This means you do not have a chance to reduce pathogens that may have gotten into the salad. Therefore, you must take a few extra steps. Follow these guidelines:

- Only use leftover TCS food, such as pasta, chicken, and potatoes, if it was cooked, held, cooled, and stored correctly.

- Do **NOT** use leftover TCS food that has been held for more than seven days. Check the use-by date of the stored TCS food before using it.

Ice

Follow these guidelines to avoid contaminating ice in your operation:

Consumption   Make ice from water that is safe to drink.

Cooling food   **NEVER** use ice as an ingredient if it was used to keep food cold. For example, if ice is used to cool food on a salad bar, it cannot then be used in drinks.

Containers and scoops   Use clean and sanitized containers and ice scoops to transfer ice from an ice machine to other containers.

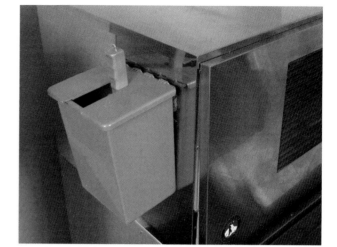

- Store ice scoops outside of the ice machine in a clean, protected location, as shown in the photo at right.

- **NEVER** hold or carry ice in containers that have held raw meat, seafood, or poultry; or chemicals.

- **NEVER** touch ice with hands or use a glass to scoop ice.

Preparation Practices That Have Special Requirements

You will need a variance when prepping food in certain ways. A variance is a document issued by your regulatory authority that allows a regulatory requirement to be waived or changed.

When applying for a variance, your regulatory authority may require you to submit a HACCP plan. The plan must account for any food safety risks related to the way you plan to prep the food item.

You will need a variance if your operation plans to prep food in any of the following ways:

- Packaging fresh juice on-site for sale at a later time, unless the juice has a warning label that complies with local regulations.

- Smoking food as a way to preserve it (but not to enhance flavor).

- Using food additives or adding components such as vinegar to preserve or alter the food so that it no longer needs time and temperature control for safety.

- Curing food.

- Custom-processing animals for personal use. For example, a hunter brings a deer to a restaurant for dressing and takes the meat home for later use.

- Packaging food using a reduced-oxygen packaging (ROP) method. This includes MAP, vacuum-packed, and sous vide food, as shown in the photo at right.

- Sprouting seeds or beans.

- Offering live shellfish from a display tank.

Apply Your Knowledge

What's the Problem?   Decide if the food in each situation was prepped correctly. Explain why or why not.

1 Marie needed to make 15 chef salads for lunch service in 3 hours. She got out the lettuce, meat, and cheese and left them on the prep table so that she could make the salads in between her other tasks.

Was the food prepped correctly? Why or why not?

_____

_____

2 Krista deveined raw shrimp on a blue cutting board for the restaurant's signature shrimp scampi. Then she washed her hands, cleaned and sanitized the prep table, and then used a different knife to slice melons on a green cutting board.

Was the food prepped correctly? Why or why not?

_____

_____

3 Jonathan filled a clean and sanitized prep sink with cold water and ice. Then he soaked a partial case of spinach that he had gotten from the cooler. Next he added a new case of spinach that was delivered that morning.

Was the food prepped correctly? Why or why not?

_____

_____

4 Jeff wanted to test whether his customers would buy fresh juice to take home. He created a special display by the cash register to store the juice on ice. He labeled each bottle with the ingredients and use-by date.

Was the food prepped correctly? Why or why not?

_____

_____

5 Phillip, the chef at a nursing home, wanted to treat the residents to his famous chocolate mousse. He whipped egg whites using pasteurized eggs whites with chocolate, cream, sugar, and vanilla and poured the mixture into individual serving dishes.

Was the food prepped correctly? Why or why not?

_____

_____

For answers, please turn to page 6.24.

Apply Your Knowledge

Pick the Correct Way to Prep Food   Write an X next to the correct answer in each pair.

1 **When using pooled eggs:**

A _____   Cook them promptly after mixing, or store them at room temperature.

B _____   Cook them promptly after mixing, or store them at 41°F (5°C) or lower.

2 **To thaw frozen food:**

A _____   Place the item in a prep sink with warm, running water.

B _____   Place the item in a cooler that keeps it at 41°F (5°C) or lower.

3 **To protect ice:**

A _____   Store ice scoops inside of the ice bin.

B _____   Store ice scoops outside of the machine in a clean, protected location.

4 **When storing leftover salads that contain TCS food:**

A _____   Throw out leftovers held at 41°F (5°C) or lower after 7 days.

B _____   Throw out leftovers held at 41°F (5°C) or lower after 10 days.

For answers, please turn to page 6.24.

Cooking Food

The only way to reduce pathogens in food to safe levels is to cook it to its correct minimum internal temperature. This temperature is different for each food. Once reached, you must hold the food at this temperature for a specific amount of time. If customers request a lower temperature, you need to inform them of the potential risk of foodborne illness. Also be aware of special menu restrictions if you serve high-risk populations.

While cooking reduces pathogens in food, it does not destroy spores or toxins they may have produced. You still must handle food correctly before you cook it.

How to Check Temperatures

To make sure the food you are cooking has reached the correct temperature, you must know how to take the temperature correctly. Follow these guidelines.

Pick a thermometer with a probe that is the correct size for the food.

Check the temperature in the thickest part of the food.

Take at least two readings in different locations.

Cooking Requirements for Specific Food

Monitor the temperature of cooked food to make sure it has reached the correct temperature. Minimum temperatures have been developed for TCS food. Most of these foods will need to be held at the minimum temperature for a minimum amount of time. These temperatures and times are listed in Table 6.2. However, your operation or area might have different requirements. *Check your local regulatory requirements.*

Table 6.2: Cooking Requirements for Specific Types of Food

165°F (74°C) for 15 seconds
- Poultry—including whole or ground chicken, turkey, or duck
- Stuffing made with fish, meat, or poultry
- Stuffed meat, seafood, poultry, or pasta
- Dishes that include previously cooked TCS ingredients (raw ingredients should be cooked to their required minimum internal temperatures)

155°F (68°C) for 15 seconds
- Ground meat—including beef, pork, and other meat
- Injected meat—including brined ham and flavor-injected roasts
- Mechanically tenderized meat
- Ratites (mostly flightless birds with flat breastbones)—including ostrich and emu
- Ground seafood—including chopped or minced seafood
- Shell eggs that will be hot held for service

145°F (63°C) for 15 seconds
- Seafood—including fish, shellfish, and crustaceans
- Steaks/chops of pork, beef, veal, and lamb
- Commercially raised game
- Shell eggs that will be served immediately

145°F (63°C) for 4 minutes
- Roasts of pork, beef, veal, and lamb
- Roasts may be cooked to these alternate cooking times and temperatures depending on the type of roast and oven used:

130°F (54°C)	112 minutes		138°F (59°C)	18 minutes
131°F (55°C)	89 minutes		140°F (60°C)	12 minutes
133°F (56°C)	56 minutes		142°F (61°C)	8 minutes
135°F (57°C)	36 minutes		144°F (62°C)	5 minutes
136°F (58°C)	28 minutes			

135°F (57°C) (no minimum time)
- Fruit, vegetables, grains (e.g., rice, pasta), and legumes (e.g., beans, refried beans) that will be hot held for service

Cooking TCS Food in the Microwave Oven

Meat, seafood, poultry, and eggs that you cook in a microwave oven must be cooked to 165°F (74°C). In addition, follow these guidelines:

- Cover the food to prevent its surface from drying out.

- Rotate or stir it halfway through the cooking process so that the heat reaches the food more evenly.

- Let the covered food stand for at least two minutes after cooking to let the food temperature even out.

- Check the temperature in at least two places to make sure that the food is cooked through.

Partial Cooking during Preparation

Some operations partially cook food during prep and then finish cooking it just before service. This is called partial cooking, or parcooking. You must follow the steps below if you plan to partially cook meat, seafood, poultry, eggs, or dishes containing these items.

1 Do not cook the food for longer than 60 minutes during initial cooking.

2 Cool the food immediately after initial cooking.

3 Freeze or refrigerate the food after cooling it. If refrigerating the food, make sure it is held at 41°F (5°C) or lower. If the food will be refrigerated, store it away from ready-to-eat food.

4 Heat the food to its required minimum internal temperature before selling or serving it.

5 Cool the food if it will not be served immediately or held for service.

Your local regulatory authority will require you to have written procedures that explain how the food cooked by this process will be prepped and stored. These procedures must be approved by the regulatory authority and describe the following:

- How the requirements will be monitored and documented
- Which corrective actions will be taken if requirements are not met
- How these food items will be marked after initial cooking to indicate that they need further cooking
- How these food items will be separated from ready-to-eat food during storage, once initial cooking is complete

Consumer Advisories

You must cook TCS food to the required minimum internal temperatures listed in this chapter unless a customer requests otherwise. This might happen often in your operation, particularly if you serve meat, eggs, or seafood.

Disclosure   If your menu includes TCS items that are raw or undercooked, such as animal products, you must note it on the menu next to these items. This can also be done by placing an asterisk next to the item that points customers to a footnote at the bottom of the menu. The footnote must include a statement that indicates the item is raw or undercooked, or contains raw or undercooked ingredients. The menu in the photo at right shows an example of disclosure.

Reminder   You must advise customers who order TCS food that is raw or undercooked, such as animal products, of the increased risk of foodborne illness. You can do this by posting a notice in your menu. You can also provide this information using brochures, table tents, signs, or other written methods. The menu here also shows an example of a reminder statement below the disclosure.

BBQ Chicken Sandwich
Chicken breast grilled with Bill's barbeque sauce, served with cheddar cheese on toasted brioche bun

Bill's Burger*   ← Disclosure
A third pound of ground beef grilled to order, served with your choice of cheese and fixin's on a toasted sesame bun

* This item is served raw or undercooked, or contains (or may contain) raw or undercooked ingredients.

Consuming raw or undercooked meats, poultry, seafood, shellfish, or eggs may increase your RISK of foodborne illness.   ← Reminder

Children's Menus

The Food and Drug Administration (FDA) advises against offering raw or undercooked meat, poultry, seafood, or eggs on a children's menu. This is especially true for undercooked ground beef, which may be contaminated with shiga toxin-producing *E. coli* O157:H7.

Operations That Mainly Serve High-Risk Populations

Operations that mainly serve a high-risk population, such as nursing homes or day-care centers, cannot serve certain items. **NEVER** serve these items:

- Raw seed sprouts.

- Raw or undercooked eggs (unpasteurized), meat, or seafood. Examples include over-easy eggs, raw oysters on the half shell, and rare hamburgers.

- Unpasteurized milk or juice.

Apply Your Knowledge

How Do You Check It? Place an X in the space that shows the correct way to check a temperature.

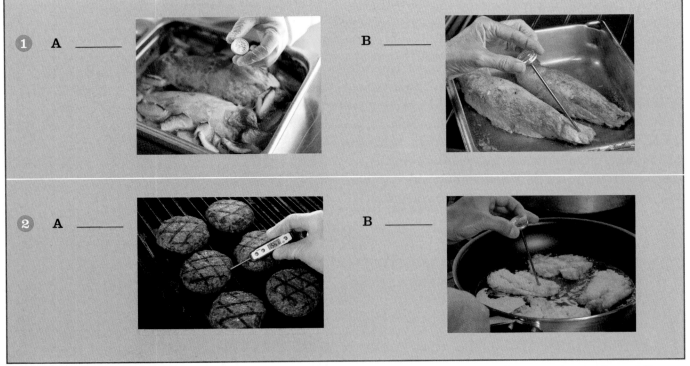

1 A _____   B _____

2 A _____   B _____

For answers, please turn to page 6.24.

Apply Your Knowledge

What's the Temperature?   Identify the required minimum internal cooking temperature for each food. Write the letter in the space provided. Some letters will be used more than once.

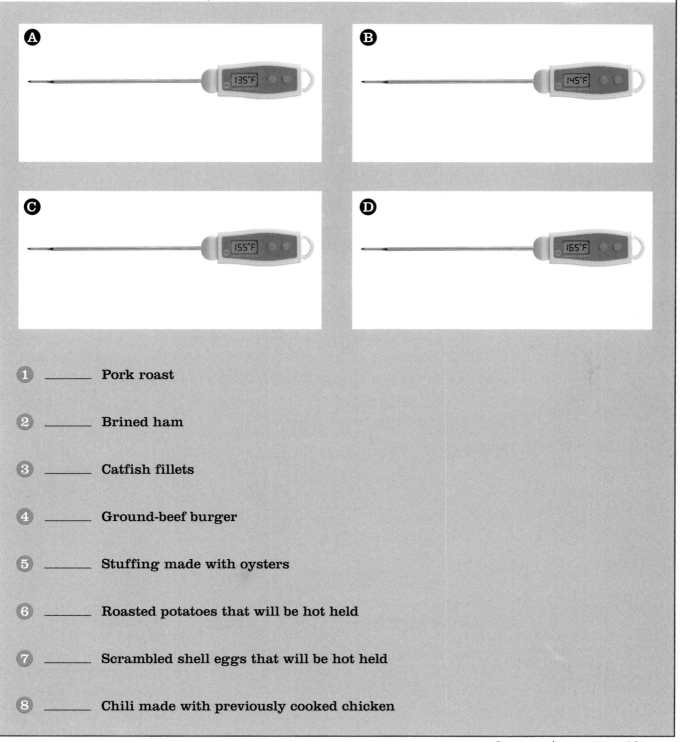

Ⓐ 135°F

Ⓑ 145°F

Ⓒ 155°F

Ⓓ 165°F

① _____ **Pork roast**

② _____ **Brined ham**

③ _____ **Catfish fillets**

④ _____ **Ground-beef burger**

⑤ _____ **Stuffing made with oysters**

⑥ _____ **Roasted potatoes that will be hot held**

⑦ _____ **Scrambled shell eggs that will be hot held**

⑧ _____ **Chili made with previously cooked chicken**

For answers, please turn to page 6.24.

Cooling and Reheating Food

When you do not serve cooked food immediately, you must get it out of the temperature danger zone as quickly as possible. That means cooling it quickly. You also need to reheat it correctly, especially if you are going to hold it.

Something to Think About

Shiga toxin-producing *E. coli* is also known as STEC. A recent STEC outbreak sickened more than 100 people who ate food containing cilantro at a popular restaurant. A health inspection after the outbreak found some critical violations. These included improper hand hygiene by workers and temperature abuse of TCS foods, including some that contained the cilantro.

Temperature Requirements for Cooling Food

As you know, pathogens grow well in the temperature danger zone. However, they grow much faster at temperatures between 125°F and 70°F (52°C and 21°C). Food must pass through this temperature range quickly to reduce this growth.

Cool TCS food from 135°F (57°C) to 41°F (5°C) or lower within six hours.

135°F (57°C)
70°F (21°C)
2 hours

First, cool food from 135°F to 70°F (57°C to 21°C) within two hours.

70°F (21°C)
41°F (5°C)
4 hours

Then cool it from 70°F to 41°F (21°C to 5°C) or lower in the next four hours.

If food has not cooled to 70°F (21°C) within two hours, it must be reheated and then cooled again.

If you can cool the food from 135°F to 70°F (57°C to 21°C) in less than two hours, you can use the remaining time to cool it to 41°F (5°C) or lower. However, the total cooling time cannot be longer than six hours. For example, if you cool food from 135°F to 70°F (57°C to 21°C) in one hour, you have the remaining five hours to get the food to 41°F (5°C) or lower.

Cooling Food

Several factors and cooling methods can affect how quickly food will cool.

Factors That Affect Cooling

The following factors affect how quickly food will cool:

Thickness or density of the food   The denser the food, the more slowly it will cool.

Size of the food   Large food items cool more slowly than smaller items. To let food cool faster, you should reduce its size. Cut large food items into smaller pieces. Divide large containers of food into smaller containers or shallow pans, as shown in the photo at right.

Storage container   Stainless steel transfers heat away from food faster than plastic. Shallow pans let the heat from food disperse faster than deep pans.

Methods for Cooling Food

NEVER cool large amounts of hot food in a cooler. Most coolers are not designed to cool large amounts of hot food quickly. Also, placing hot food in a cooler may not move the food through the temperature danger zone quickly enough. Here are some effective methods for cooling food quickly and safely:

Ice-water bath   After dividing food into smaller containers, place them in a clean prep sink or large pot filled with ice water. The food handler in the photo at right is cooling a container of meat sauce this way.

Stir the food frequently to cool it faster and more evenly.

Study Questions

Circle the best answer to each question.

1 **Why must prep tables be cleaned and sanitized between uses?**

   A   To make space to work safely

   B   To prevent cross-contamination

   C   To reduce toxic-metal poisoning

   D   To avoid time-temperature abuse

2 **What should happen to food right after it is thawed in a microwave oven?**

   A   Freeze it solid.

   B   Cool it to 41°F (5°C).

   C   Cook it in conventional cooking equipment.

   D   Hold it in equipment that maintains the correct temperature.

3 **When cooling TCS food, the temperature must go from 135°F to 70°F (57°C to 21°C) in**

   A   2 hours.

   B   4 hours.

   C   6 hours.

   D   8 hours.

4 **A food handler left a hotel pan of pasta salad on the prep table while preparing several lunch orders. What is the problem with this situation?**

   A   Cross-contamination

   B   Poor personal hygiene

   C   Time-temperature abuse

   D   Poor cleaning and sanitizing

5 **What is the maximum water temperature allowed when thawing food under running water?**

   A   41°F (5°C)

   B   60°F (16°C)

   C   70°F (21°C)

   D   135°F (57°C)

Study Questions

6 **What is the required minimum internal cooking temperature for ground turkey?**

    A   135°F (57°C) for 15 seconds

    B   145°F (63°C) for 15 seconds

    C   155°F (68°C) for 15 seconds

    (D) 165°F (74°C) for 15 seconds

7 **A safe way to cool a stockpot of meat sauce is to put it into a**

    A   cooler.

    B   freezer.

    (C) sink of ice water.

    D   cold-holding unit.

8 **Which food item should not be served to high-risk populations?**

    A   Vegetable stir-fry

    B   Grilled salmon

    C   Roasted chicken

    (D) Raw oysters

9 **To what temperature must soup that contains cooked beef be reheated for hot holding?**

    A   135°F (57°C) for 15 seconds

    B   145°F (63°C) for 15 seconds

    C   155°F (68°C) for 15 seconds

    D   165°F (74°C) for 15 seconds

10 **When partially cooking food for later service, what is the maximum amount of time that the food can be heated during the initial cooking step?**

    (A) 60 minutes

    B   70 minutes

    C   80 minutes

    D   90 minutes

For answers, please turn to page 6.25.

Answers

6.8 What's the Problem?

1 No. The lettuce, meat, and cheese are being time-temperature abused. She should take out of the cooler only what she can use within a short amount of time.

2 Yes. She used separate equipment for the shrimp and the produce.

3 No. One batch of spinach could cross-contaminate the other. Between batches, he should have emptied the sink, cleaned and sanitized it, and changed the ice water.

4 No. He should have either gotten a variance from his local regulatory authority before selling the juice without a warning label or included warning labels on the juice.

5 Yes. He used pasteurized eggs because raw shell eggs and undercooked, unpasteurized shell eggs cannot be served in a nursing home.

6.9 Pick the Correct Way to Prep Food

1 B
2 B
3 B
4 A

6.14 How Do You Check It?

1 A
2 A

6.15 What's the Temperature?

1 B   5 D
2 C   6 A
3 B   7 C
4 C   8 D

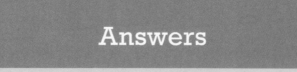

Answers

6.19 Cooling Food

1 and 2 should be marked.

6.19 Is It Hot Enough?

1 No. The chili did not reach an internal temperature of 165°F (74°C) within two hours.

2 Yes. Assuming the roast beef was cooked and cooled correctly, it can be reheated to any temperature because it is being served immediately.

6.21 Chapter Review Case Study

1 Here is what Amanda did wrong:

- She thawed the chicken breasts the wrong way. She should not have thawed them under hot water.

- She cooled the leftover chicken breasts the wrong way. She should not have left them out to cool at room temperature.

- She did not make sure that the clam chowder reached at least 165°F (75°C) for 15 seconds.

2 Here is what Amanda should have done differently:

- If Amanda needed to thaw the chicken breasts quickly, she should have either used a microwave or placed them under running water at 70°F (21°C) or lower.

- Amanda should have ensured the clam chowder was heated to at least 165°F (75°C) for 15 seconds before moving it to the steam table.

- To cool the chicken breasts, she could have used a blast chiller or placed the container of chicken breasts in an ice-water bath. Then she could move them to the cooler.

6.22 Study Questions

1	B	6	D
2	C	7	C
3	A	8	D
4	C	9	D
5	C	10	A

Holding Food

Food that is being held for service is at risk for time-temperature abuse and cross-contamination. If your operation holds food, you must make policies that reduce these risks. Focus on time and temperature control, but do not forget about protecting the food from contamination. In some cases, you might be able to hold food without controlling its temperature.

Guidelines for Holding Food

Create policies about how long the operation will hold food. Also, create policies about when to throw away held food. For example, your policy may let you refill a pan of veal in a buffet all day, as long as you throw it out at the end of the day. Policies should also consider the following.

Food covers and sneeze guards Cover food and install sneeze guards to protect food from contaminants. Covers, like the ones shown in the photo at left, also help maintain a food's internal temperature.

Temperature Hold TCS food at the correct internal temperature:

* Hold hot food at 135°F (57°C) or higher.
* Hold cold food at 41°F (5°C) or lower.

Thermometer Use a thermometer to check a food's internal temperature. **NEVER** use the temperature gauge on a holding unit to check the food's temperature. The gauge does not check the internal temperature of the food.

Time Check food temperatures at least every four hours, as shown in the photo at left. Follow these guidelines:

* Throw out food that is not 41°F (5°C) or lower or 135°F (57°C) or higher.
* You can also check the temperature every two hours. This will leave time for corrective action. For example, hot TCS food that has been held below 135°F (57°C) can be reheated and then placed back in the hot-holding unit.

Hot-holding equipment **NEVER** use hot-holding equipment to reheat food unless it is built to do so. Most hot-holding equipment does not pass food through the temperature danger zone quickly enough. Reheat food correctly. Then move it to the holding unit.

Holding Food without Temperature Control

Your operation may want to display or hold TCS food without temperature control. However, if you primarily serve a high-risk population, you cannot hold TCS food without temperature control.

Here are some examples of when food might be held without temperature control:

- When displaying food for a short time, such as at an off-site catered event, as shown in the photo at right

- When electricity is not available to power holding equipment

If your operation displays or holds TCS food without temperature control, it must do so under certain conditions. Also note that the conditions for holding cold food are different from those for holding hot food.

Before using time as a method of control, check with your local regulatory authority for specific requirements.

Cold Food

You can hold cold food without temperature control for up to six hours if you meet these conditions:

- Hold the food at 41°F (5°C) or lower before removing it from refrigeration.

- Label the food with the time you removed it from refrigeration and the time you must throw it out. The discard time on the label must be six hours from the time you removed the food from refrigeration, as shown in the photo at right. For example, if you remove potato salad from refrigeration at 3:00 p.m. to serve at a picnic, the discard time on the label should be 9:00 p.m. This equals six hours from the time you removed it from refrigeration.

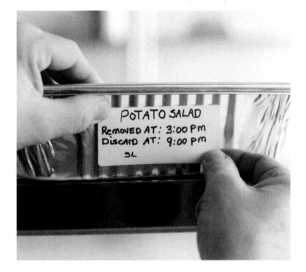

- Make sure the food temperature does not exceed 70°F (21°C) while it is being served. Throw out any food that exceeds this temperature.

- Sell, serve, or throw out the food within six hours.

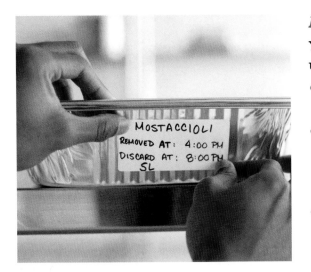

Hot Food

You can hold hot food without temperature control for up to four hours if you meet these conditions:

- Hold the food at 135°F (57°C) or higher before removing it from temperature control.

- Label the food with the time you must throw it out. The discard time on the label must be four hours from the time you removed the food from temperature control, as shown in the photo at left.

- Sell, serve, or throw out the food within four hours.

Apply Your Knowledge

Is It Being Handled Safely?   Write an X next to each food item that is not being handled safely.

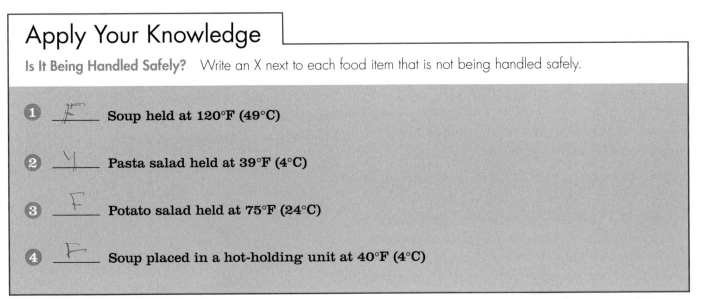

1. _____ Soup held at 120°F (49°C)

2. _____ Pasta salad held at 39°F (4°C)

3. _____ Potato salad held at 75°F (24°C)

4. _____ Soup placed in a hot-holding unit at 40°F (4°C)

For answers, please turn to page 7.18.

Apply Your Knowledge

Is It Safe?   Read each story and decide if the food is safe to serve. Explain why or why not in the space provided. Assume the food has been correctly labeled.

1 Roy prepared pans of pasta with meat sauce and held them in a 200°F (93°C) degree oven for two hours. At 5:00 p.m., he packed them in an insulated container to take to a wedding reception at the beach. There was no equipment to keep the food hot. At 8:00 p.m., three hours after Roy removed the pasta from the oven in his operation, the pasta was served to the guests.

_____

_____

_____

_____

2 At 6:00 a.m., Alvin removed deli meat, sliced cheese, apples, and pudding cups from the cooler to make box lunches for a high school class field trip. When he finished making the lunches, Alvin left them on a table for the teacher. The lunches were left on the bus that warm spring day while the students toured a museum. At 1:00 p.m., they returned to a very warm bus to get their lunches, which they ate in a picnic area.

_____

_____

_____

_____

3 Sally is a cook at the Springfield Retirement Community. As a special treat, she set up a picnic for some of the elderly residents. The picnic included a buffet of cold chicken, potato salad, coleslaw, rolls, and cupcakes. There was no equipment to keep the food cold. The food was served one hour after it was removed from the cooler.

_____

_____

_____

_____

For answers, please turn to page 7.18.

Serving Food

The biggest threat to food that is ready to be served is contamination. Your kitchen and service staff must know how to serve food in ways that keep it safe. Dining rooms, self-service areas, off-site locations, and vending machines all have specific guidelines that staff must follow.

Kitchen Staff Guidelines

Train your kitchen staff to serve food in these ways.

Bare-hand contact with food   Food handlers must wear single-use gloves whenever handling ready-to-eat food. As an alternative, food can be handled with spatulas, tongs, deli sheets, or other utensils. The photo at left shows two ways to avoid bare-hand contact. Keep in mind that there are some situations where it may be acceptable to handle ready-to-eat food with bare hands. These were discussed earlier.

Clean and sanitized utensils   Use separate utensils for each food item. Clean and sanitize them after each serving task. If using utensils continuously, clean and sanitize them at least once every four hours.

Serving utensils   Store serving utensils in the food with the handle extended above the rim of the container, as shown in the photo at left. Or if you are serving a non-TCS food item, you can place them on a clean and sanitized food-contact surface. Spoons or scoops used to serve food such as ice cream or mashed potatoes can be stored under running water. They can also be stored in a container of water that is maintained at a temperature of at least 135°F (57°C).

Refilling take-home containers   Some jurisdictions allow food handlers to refill take-home containers brought back by a guest with food and beverages. Take-home containers can be refilled if they meet these conditions:

- They were designed to be reused.
- They were provided to the guest by the operation.
- They are cleaned and sanitized correctly.

Take-home beverage containers can also be refilled as long as the beverage is not a TCS food and the container will be refilled for the same guest. The container must also meet these conditions:

- It can be effectively cleaned at home and in the operation.
- It will be rinsed with fresh, hot water under pressure before refilling.
- It will be refilled by staff in the operation or by the guest using a process that prevents contamination.

Service Staff Guidelines

Service staff must be as careful as kitchen staff. They can contaminate food simply by handling the food-contact areas of glasses, dishes, and utensils. Service staff should use these guidelines when serving food.

- Hold dishes by the bottom or edge.
- Hold glasses by the middle, bottom, or stem.
- Do **NOT** touch the food-contact areas of dishes or glassware.

- Carry glasses in a rack or on a tray to avoid touching the food-contact surfaces.
- Do **NOT** stack glasses when carrying them.

- Hold flatware by the handle.
- Do **NOT** hold flatware by food-contact surfaces.
- Store flatware so that servers grasp handles, not food-contact surfaces.

Continued on following page.

- Avoid bare-hand contact with food that is ready to eat.

- Use ice scoops or tongs to get ice.

- **NEVER** scoop ice with your bare hands or a glass. A glass may chip or break.

Something to Think About

Nearly 100 people became sick and more than 20 were hospitalized after attending a catered wedding reception. An investigation found *Salmonella* in the cooked chicken and green beans. An official stated that the initial source of the *Salmonella* was the chicken. The green beans were likely contaminated by a shared serving utensil.

Preset Tableware

If your operation presets tableware on dining tables, you must take steps to prevent it from becoming contaminated. This might include wrapping or covering the items, as shown in the photo at right.

Table settings do not need to be wrapped or covered if extra or unused settings meet these requirements:

- They are removed when guests are seated.
- If they remain on the table, they are cleaned and sanitized after guests have left.

Re-serving Food

Service and kitchen staff should also know the rules about re-serving food that was previously served to another guest.

Menu items   Do **NOT** re-serve food returned by one guest to another guest.

Condiments   You must protect condiments from contamination. Serve them in their original containers or in containers designed to prevent contamination. Offering condiments in individual packets or portions can also help keep them safe.

- **NEVER** re-serve uncovered condiments.
- Do **NOT** combine leftover condiments with fresh ones, like the food handler in the photo at right is doing.
- Throw away opened portions or dishes of condiments after serving them to guests. Salsa, butter, mayonnaise, and ketchup are examples.

Bread or rolls   Do **NOT** re-serve uneaten bread to other guests. Change linens used in bread baskets after each guest.

Garnishes   **NEVER** re-serve plate garnishes, such as fruit or pickles, to another guest. Throw out served but unused garnishes.

Prepackaged food   In general, you may re-serve only unopened, prepackaged food in good condition. These include condiment packets and wrapped crackers. You may re-serve bottles of ketchup, mustard, and other condiments. The containers must remain closed between uses.

Self-Service Areas

Self-service areas can be contaminated easily. Follow these guidelines to prevent contamination and time-temperature abuse.

Protection   Food on display can be protected from contamination using sneeze guards. Food can also be protected by placing it in display cases or by packaging it in a way that will protect it from contamination. Whole, raw fruits and vegetables and nuts in the shell that require peeling or hulling before eating do not require the protection measures discussed above.

Labels   Label food located in self-service areas. For example, place the name of the food, such as types of salad dressing, on ladle handles or signs, as shown in the photo at left.

Temperature   Keep hot food hot at 135°F (57°C) or higher. Keep cold food cold at 41°F (5°C) or lower.

Raw and ready-to-eat food   Typically, raw, unpackaged meat, poultry, and seafood cannot be offered for self-service. However, these items are an exception:

- Ready-to-eat food at buffets or salad bars that serve food such as sushi or raw shellfish
- Ready-to-cook portions that will be cooked and eaten immediately on the premises, such as at Mongolian barbecues
- Raw, frozen, shell-on shrimp or lobster

Refills   Do **NOT** let guests refill dirty plates or use dirty utensils at self-service areas. Pathogens such as Norovirus can easily be transferred by reused plates and utensils. Assign a staff member to monitor guests. Post signs reminding guests not to reuse plates and utensils.

Utensils   Stock food displays with the correct utensils for dispensing food. This might include tongs, ladles, or deli sheets.

Ice   Ice used to keep food or beverages cold should **NEVER** be used as an ingredient.

Labeling Bulk Food

Bulk food in self-service areas must be labeled. The label must be in plain view of the guest. When labeling food, you can include the manufacturer or processor label provided with the food. As an alternative, you can provide this information using a card, sign, or other labeling method.

Bulk unpackaged food, such as bakery products and unpackaged food portioned for customers, does not need to be labeled if it meets these conditions:

* The product makes no claim regarding health or nutrient content.

* There are no laws requiring labeling.

* The food is manufactured or prepared on the premises.

* The food is manufactured or prepared at another food operation or processing plant owned by the same person. The operation must also be regulated.

Off-Site Service

Delays from the point of preparation to the point of service increase the risk that food will be exposed to contamination or time-temperature abuse. To transport food and items correctly, follow these procedures.

Food containers   Pack food in insulated food containers. Use only food-grade containers, such as those shown in the photo at right. They should be designed so food cannot mix, leak, or spill. At the service site, use appropriate containers or equipment to hold food at the correct temperature.

Labels   Label food with a use-by date and time, and reheating and service instructions for staff at off-site locations. This is shown in the photo at right.

Delivery vehicles   Clean the inside of delivery vehicles regularly.

Internal temperature   Check internal food temperatures. If containers or delivery vehicles are not holding food at the correct temperature, reevaluate the length of the delivery route or the efficiency of the equipment being used.

Utilities   Make sure the service site has the correct utilities:

* Safe water for cooking, dishwashing, and handwashing

* Garbage containers stored away from food-prep, storage, and serving areas

Storage   Store raw meat, poultry, and seafood separate from ready-to-eat items. For example, store raw chicken separate from ready-to-eat salads.

Vending Machines

Handle food prepped and packaged for vending machines with the same care as any other food served to guests. Vending operators should protect food from contamination and time-temperature abuse during transport, delivery, and service. To keep vended food safe, follow these guidelines:

Turkey & Cheese Sandwich
See side panel or insert for ingredient information.
ABC Vending Co.
Chicago IL 60604

SELL BY 03/30   NET WT 6.75oz (191g)

- Check product shelf life daily. Products often have a code date, such as an expiration or use-by date, like that shown in the photo at left. If the date has expired, throw out the food immediately. Throw out refrigerated food prepped on-site if not sold within seven days of preparation.

- Keep TCS food at the correct temperature. It should be held at 41°F (5°C) or lower, or at 135°F (57°C) or higher. These machines must have controls that prevent TCS food from being dispensed if the temperature stays in the danger zone for a specified amount of time. This food must be thrown out.

- Dispense TCS food in its original container.

- Wash and wrap fresh fruit with edible peels before putting it in a machine.

Apply Your Knowledge

Re-serve or Throw Out?   Write a T next to the food that you must throw out. Write an R next to the items you can re-serve.

1. __T__ Chili held without temperature control for five hours

2. __T__ Previously served, but untouched, basket of bread

3. __R__ Bottle of ketchup with cap on

4. __T__ Untouched slice of pie with whipped cream returned by a customer

5. __T__ Individually wrapped crackers

6. __R__ Unwrapped butter served on a plate

7. __T__ Mustard packets

8. __T__ Ice used to hold cold food on a self-service area

9. __T__ Breaded, baked fish returned by a customer who wanted broiled fish

10. __R__ A washed and wrapped pear that has been in a vending machine for eight days

For answers, please turn to page 7.18.

Apply Your Knowledge

Is It Being Served Safely?   Write an X next to each food item that is not being served safely.

1 _____

2 _____

3 _____

4 _____

5 _____

6 _____

For answers, please turn to page 7.18.

Chapter Summary

- Your operation should have policies for holding and discarding food. Cover food or use sneeze guards. Hold TCS food at the correct temperature. Use a thermometer to check the internal temperature at least every four hours. Never use hot-holding equipment to reheat food unless it is built to do so.

- When holding TCS food for service, keep hot food at 135°F (57°C) or higher. Keep cold food at 41°F (5°C) or lower. Check the internal temperature of food at least every four hours. Throw food out if it is not at the correct temperature and cannot be restored to a safe condition.

- TCS food may be held without temperature control under certain conditions. Cold food must be held at 41°F (5°C) or lower before it is removed from refrigeration. Then, the food temperature must not get higher than 70°F (21°C). If it does, or if the food is not served or sold within six hours, the food must be thrown away. Hot food must be held at 135°F (57°C) or higher before it is removed from temperature control. Then it must be served, stored, or thrown away within four hours. Both cold and hot food must be labeled with the discard time. Operations that primarily serve high-risk populations should never hold food without temperature control.

- In general, staff should be trained to avoid bare-hand contact with ready-to-eat food. They should also be trained to use and maintain utensils correctly. Use separate utensils for different food items. Clean and sanitize them after each task and after four hours of continuous use. Store serving utensils correctly to avoid contamination. Follow guidelines for refilling take-home containers.

- Teach staff the correct ways for handling service items and tableware. Staff should also be trained on the rules for throwing away and re-serving food that was served to customers. This should address food returned by customers and unused condiments, bread, garnishes, and prepackaged food.

- Self-service areas can be contaminated by staff and customers. Protect food on display with sneeze guards, packaging, or other tools designed to keep food safe. Post self-service rules. Make it clear to customers that clean plates must be used for refills. Put the correct labels on displayed food and bulk food available for self-service. Make sure equipment holds food at the correct temperature.

- Follow safety procedures when prepping, delivering, or serving food off-site. Pack food in insulated, food-grade containers. Make sure food cannot mix, leak, or spill. Label food with the use-by date and time and reheating and service instructions. Store raw meat, poultry, and seafood separate from ready-to-eat items. Make sure delivery vehicles are clean and holding equipment keeps food at the correct temperature. Make sure the service site has the correct utilities.

- Vending machine food should be handled as carefully as any other food. Check product shelf life daily. Hold TCS food at the correct temperature.

Chapter Review Case Study

To keep food safe during holding and serving, you must know how to hold hot and cold food; use time as a method of control to hold food; and prevent contamination of food in self-service areas and when serving food to customers.

Now, take what you have learned in this chapter and apply it to the following case study.

Jill, a line cook on the morning shift at Memorial Hospital, was also filling in for the kitchen manager, who usually supervises lunch in the cafeteria. Jill was also responsible for making sure meals were trayed and put into food carts for transport to the patients' rooms. The staff also packed two dozen meals each day for a neighborhood group that delivered them to homebound elderly people.

Knowing the delivery driver would arrive soon to pick up the meals, Jill looked for insulated food containers to hold them. When she could not find any, she loaded the meals into cardboard boxes she found near the back door. The cafeteria was busy, and the staff had many meals to tray and deliver.

As the lunch period was ending, Jill breathed a sigh of relief. She moved down the cafeteria serving line, checking food temperatures. One of the casseroles was at 130°F (54°C). Jill checked the water level in the steam table and turned up the thermostat. She then went to clean up the kitchen and finish her shift.

1 What did Jill do wrong?

_____

_____

_____

_____

2 What should Jill have done?

_____

_____

_____

_____

For answers, please turn to page 7.19.

Study Questions

Circle the best answer to each question.

1 Which part of the plate should a food handler avoid touching when serving customers?

A Bottom

B Edge

C Side

D Top

2 An operation has a self-service salad bar with 8 different items on it. How many serving utensils are needed to serve the items on the salad bar?

A 2

B 4

C 6

D 8

3 At what maximum internal temperature should cold TCS food be held?

A 0°F (-17°C)

B 32°F (0°C)

C 41°F (5°C)

D 60°F (16°C)

4 What item must customers take each time they return to a self-service area for more food?

A Clean plate

B Extra napkins

C Hand sanitizer

D New serving spoon

5 At what minimum internal temperature should hot TCS food be held?

A 115°F (46°C)

B 125°F (52°C)

C 135°F (57°C)

D 145°F (63°C)

Study Questions

6 An operation is located in a jurisdiction that allows it to hold TCS food without temperature control. How many hours can it display hot TCS food without temperature control before the food must be sold, served, or thrown out?

   A 2

   B 4

   C 6

   D 8

7 How often must you check the temperature of food that is being held with temperature control?

   A At least every 2 hours

   B At least every 4 hours

   C At least every 6 hours

   D At least every 8 hours

8 A pan of lasagna at 165°F (74°C) was packed in a heated cabinet for off-site delivery. What is the minimum information that should be on the pan label?

   A Use-by date and time and reheating and service instructions

   B Use-by date and reheating and service instructions

   C Use-by time and reheating and service instructions

   D Use-by date and time and reheating instructions

9 Which may be handled with bare hands?

   A Cooked pasta for salad

   B Chopped potatoes for soup

   C Canned tuna for sandwiches

   D Pickled watermelon for garnish

10 When a utensil is stored in water between uses, what are the requirements?

   A Running water at any temperature, or a container of water at 70°F (21°C) or lower

   B Running water at any temperature, or a container of water at 135°F (57°C) or higher

   C Running water at 70°F (21°C) or lower, or a container of water at 70°F (21°C) or lower

   D Running water at 135°F (57°C) or higher, or a container of water at 135°F (57°C) or higher

For answers, please turn to page 7.19.

Answers

7.4   Is It Being Handled Safely?

1, 3, and 4 should be marked.

7.5   Is It Safe?

1 Yes. The food was held above 135°F (57°C) and then served within four hours after being removed from temperature control.

2 No. The lunches were left too long outside of temperature control. The temperature of the food also probably rose higher than 70°F (21°C) as the bus warmed in the sun.

3 No. Food cannot be held without temperature control if it is primarily for high-risk populations, such as elderly people.

7.12   Re-serve or Throw Out?

1 T
2 T
3 R
4 T
5 R
6 T
7 R
8 T
9 T
10 R

7.13   Is It Being Served Safely?

1, 2, 3, 4, 5, and 6 should be marked.

Answers

7.15 Chapter Review Case Study

Here is what Jill did wrong:

- She packed the deliveries in cardboard boxes instead of food-grade, insulated containers.

- She did not make sure that the internal temperature of the food on the steam table was checked at least every four hours. Then she would have known that the steam table was not maintaining the correct temperature and the casserole was in the temperature danger zone.

Here is what Jill should have done:

- She should have kept the delivery meals in a hot-holding cabinet or left the food in a steam table until suitable containers were found or the driver arrived.

- She should have thrown out the casserole and any other food that was not at the correct temperature, because she did not know how long the food was in the temperature danger zone.

7.16 Study Questions

1 D
2 D
3 C
4 A
5 C
6 B
7 B
8 A
9 B
10 B

Food Safety Management Systems

In chapters 4 through 7, you learned how to handle food safely throughout the flow of food. Now, you will learn how all of it can be applied to a food safety management system. To do this, you must understand how a food safety management system works.

Overview of Food Safety Management Systems

A food safety management system is a group of practices and procedures intended to prevent foodborne illness. It does this by actively controlling risks and hazards throughout the flow of food.

Having some food safety programs already in place gives you the foundation for your system. The principles presented in ServSafe are the basis of these programs. Here are some examples of the programs your operation needs.

Personal hygiene program	Food safety training program
Supplier selection and specification program	Quality control and assurance programs
Cleaning and sanitation program	Standard operating procedures (SOPs)
Facility design and equipment maintenance program	Pest-control program

Active Managerial Control

Earlier, you learned that there are five common risk factors for foodborne illness:

1 Purchasing food from unsafe sources

2 Failing to cook food correctly

3 Holding food at incorrect temperatures

4 Using contaminated equipment

5 Practicing poor personal hygiene

It is the manager's responsibility to actively control these and other risk factors for foodborne illness. This is called active managerial control. It is important to note that active managerial control is proactive rather than reactive. You must anticipate risks and plan for them.

There are many ways to achieve active managerial control in the operation. According to the Food and Drug Administration (FDA), you can use simple tools such as training programs, manager supervision, and the incorporation of SOPs. Active managerial control can also be achieved through more complex solutions, such as a Hazard Analysis Critical Control Point (HACCP) program.

Managers should practice active managerial control throughout the flow of food. This includes anticipating potential foodborne illness risk factors and then controlling or eliminating them. You might already do some of these things, such as purchasing food from approved suppliers. But, it also includes many of the things you have learned. For example, making sure food is held at the proper temperature or cooking food to its minimum internal cooking temperature. Monitoring the entire flow of food will help keep your customers and operation free from risk. You also must provide your staff with the proper tools, such as procedures and training to make sure food is safe.

There are some important steps to take when implementing active managerial control in your operation:

1 Identify Risks   Find and document the potential foodborne-illness risks in your operation. Then, identify the hazards that can be controlled or eliminated.

2 Monitor   Food will be safe if managers monitor critical activities in the operation. So make note of where employees must monitor food-safety requirements. This might include identifying when temperatures should be taken or how often sanitizer concentrations should be tested in a three-compartment sink. For example, the manager at left is monitoring a food handler as she carries out the critical task of cooling food correctly.

3 Corrective Action   Take the appropriate steps to correct improper procedures or behaviors. For example, if a sanitizer level is too low when tested, the situation might be corrected by increasing the concentration level.

4 Management Oversight   Verify that all policies, procedures, and corrective actions are followed.

5 Training   Ensure employees are trained to follow procedures and retrained when necessary.

6 Re-evaluation   Periodically assess the system to make sure it is working correctly and effectively.

Something to Think About

The manager of a quick service restaurant noticed that the grill operator handling raw chicken fillets also put cooked fillets in a holding drawer. The sandwich maker then touched the handle of the drawer each time she retrieved a cooked fillet—allowing for potential cross-contamination with the raw and cooked chicken. The manager decided to add an extra handle to the holding drawer. The manager then assigned the grill operator and sandwich maker their own handle.

The FDA's Public Health Interventions

The FDA provides specific recommendations for controlling the common risk factors for foodborne illness. These are known as public health interventions. They are designed to protect public health.

Demonstration of knowledge   As a manager, you must be able to show that you know what to do to keep food safe. Becoming certified in food safety is one way to show this.

Staff health controls   Procedures must be put in place to make sure staff are practicing personal hygiene. For example, staff must know that they are required to report illnesses and illness symptoms to management.

Controlling hands as a vehicle of contamination   Controls must be put in place to prevent bare-hand contact with ready-to-eat food. This might include requiring the use of tongs to handle ready-to-eat food, as shown in the photo at right.

Time and temperature parameters for controlling pathogens   Procedures must be put in place to limit the time food spends in the temperature danger zone. Requiring food handlers to check the temperature of food being hot-held every two hours is an example.

Consumer advisories   Notices must be provided to customers if you serve raw or undercooked menu items. These notices must include a statement about the risks of eating these foods.

Apply Your Knowledge

Identify the Risk   Match the example to the correct risk factor for foodborne illness.

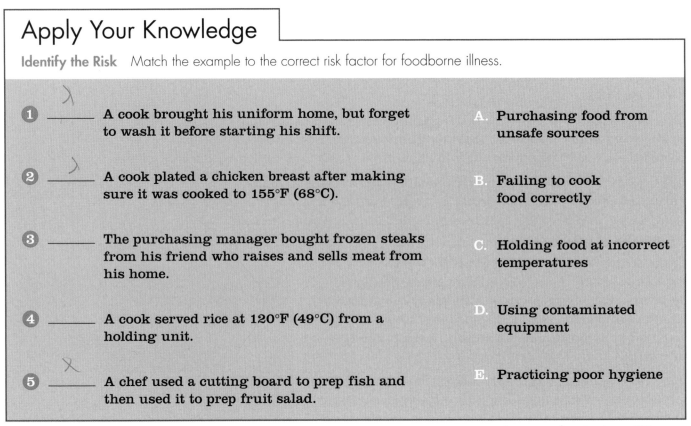

1 _____ A cook brought his uniform home, but forget to wash it before starting his shift.

2 _____ A cook plated a chicken breast after making sure it was cooked to 155°F (68°C).

3 _____ The purchasing manager bought frozen steaks from his friend who raises and sells meat from his home.

4 _____ A cook served rice at 120°F (49°C) from a holding unit.

5 _____ A chef used a cutting board to prep fish and then used it to prep fruit salad.

A. Purchasing food from unsafe sources

B. Failing to cook food correctly

C. Holding food at incorrect temperatures

D. Using contaminated equipment

E. Practicing poor hygiene

For answers, please turn to page 8.11.

HACCP

There are many systems you can implement to achieve active managerial control of foodborne-illness risk factors. A Hazard Analysis Critical Control Point (HACCP) program is one such system. A HACCP (pronounced HASS-ip) system is based on identifying significant biological, chemical, or physical hazards at specific points within a product's flow. Once identified, the hazards can be prevented, eliminated, or reduced to safe levels.

An effective HACCP system must be based on a written plan. This plan must be specific to each facility's menu, customers, equipment, processes, and operations. Because each HACCP plan is unique, a plan that works for one operation may not work for another.

Chapter Summary

- A food safety management system is a group of procedures and practices intended to prevent foodborne illness. It does this by actively controlling risks and hazards throughout the flow of food.

- It is the manager's responsibility to actively control the risk factors for foodborne illness. This is called active managerial control. It can be achieved by incorporating specific actions and procedures into the operation to prevent foodborne illness.

- There are six important steps to take when implementing active managerial control into your operation: identify risks, monitor, corrective action, management oversight, training, and re-evaluation.

- The FDA provides specific recommendations for controlling the common risk factors for foodborne illness. These are known as public health interventions. They are designed to protect public health.

- HACCP systems are based on identifying significant biological, chemical, or physical hazards at specific points within a product's flow. Once identified, the hazards can be prevented, eliminated, or reduced to safe levels.

Chapter Review Case Study

You can address food safety risks in your operation by creating a food safety management system.

Now, take what you have learned in this chapter and apply it to the following case study.

Carolyn, a new manager for Bobo's Bistro, felt a lot of pressure from her district manager to do well. Carolyn thought she could save money by purchasing produce from her friend, who has a large garden in his yard. This would save a couple hundred dollars per month. She placed an order for delivery the next day. Next, she walked around the restaurant to make sure everything was going to be ready for the dinner rush. She noticed the cook took the temperature of salmon as it came out of the oven. It read 125°F (52°C). Carolyn then checked the soups that were in the hot-holding wells. She took the temperature of the lobster bisque, which she did every two hours, and it read 105°F (41°C). She asked the lead cook, Tom, to reheat the soup.

Carolyn walked past Eddie, who was prepping ground beef for burgers. She noticed he did not have a hat on and his apron looked very dirty. She asked Eddie to put on a clean apron. Carolyn was finally finished making her rounds and started back to her office when she saw Eddie switch from prepping burgers to making Caesar salads. He was using the same cutting board and knife to prep the lettuce. She told Eddie to wash, rinse, and sanitize the cutting board and to toss any lettuce that he already cut. She thought it would probably be best to conduct a quick training session on cross-contamination for all staff.

1 What did Carolyn do correctly?

_____

_____

_____

_____

2 What did Carolyn do incorrectly?

_____

_____

_____

_____

For answers, please turn to page 8.11.

Study Questions

Circle the best answer to each question.

1 A manager's responsibility to actively control risk factors for foodborne illnesses is called

   A   hazard analysis critical control point (HACCP).

   B   quality control and assurance.

   C   food safety management.

   D   active managerial control.

2 A pest-control program is an example of a(n)

   A   HACCP program.

   B   workplace safety program.

   C   food safety program.

   D   active managerial control program.

3 A cook preps a beef tenderloin on a cutting board and then immediately cuts pies for dessert on the same cutting board. This is an example of which risk factor?

   A   Purchasing food from unsafe sources

   B   Holding food at incorrect temperatures

   C   Using contaminated equipment

   D   Practicing poor personal hygiene

4 The purpose of a food safety management system is to

   A   keep all areas of the facility clean and pest-free.

   B   identify, tag, and repair faulty equipment within the facility.

   C   prevent foodborne illness by controlling risks and hazards.

   D   use the correct methods for purchasing and receiving food.

5 Three components of active managerial control include

   A   identifying risks, creating specifications, and training.

   B   identifying risks, corrective action, and training.

   C   identifying risks, creating purchase orders, and training.

   D   identifying risks, record keeping, and training.

Study Questions

6 A manager asks a chef to continue cooking chicken breasts after seeing them cooked to an incorrect temperature. This is an example of which step in active managerial control?

A Identifying risks

B Monitoring

C Corrective action

D Re-evaluation

7 A manager walks around the kitchen every hour to answer questions and to see if staff members are following procedures. This is an example of which step in active managerial control?

A Identify risks

B Corrective action

C Management oversight

D Re-evaluation

8 One way for managers to show that they know how to keep food safe is to

A become certified in food safety.

B take cooking temperatures.

C monitor employee behaviors.

D conduct self-inspections.

For answers, please turn to page 8.11.

Answers

8.6 Identify the Risk

1 E
2 B
3 A
4 C
5 D

8.8 Chapter Review Case Study

What did Carolyn do correctly?

* She asked the lead cook to reheat the soup.
* She asked the prep cook to put on a clean apron.
* She asked the prep cook to use a clean cutting board and knife.
* She asked the prep cook to throw out the contaminated lettuce.

What did Carolyn do incorrectly?

* She purchased food from a friend instead of an approved, reputable supplier.
* She should have had the chef cook the salmon longer, to the correct minimum internal temperature.
* She should have told the prep cook to put a hair restraint on.

8.9 Study Questions

1 D
2 C
3 C
4 C
5 B
6 C
7 C
8 A

Interior Requirements for a Safe Operation

The materials, equipment, and utilities in your operation play a part in keeping food safe. Given the opportunity, you should choose these items with food safety in mind. It is also important to recognize that you may need to consult your local regulatory agency before making changes to your operation, including the facility or equipment.

Floors, Walls, and Ceilings

When choosing flooring, wall, and ceiling materials, pick those that are smooth and durable. This makes cleaning easier.

Once installed, flooring, walls, and ceilings must be regularly maintained. Replace missing or broken ceiling tiles. Do the same for flooring. Repair all holes in walls.

Floors should have coving. Coving is a curved, sealed edge between a floor and a wall. It gets rid of sharp corners or gaps that are hard to clean. Coving should be glued tightly to the wall to get rid of hiding places for insects. This also protects the wall from moisture.

If standing water occurs due to spraying or when flushing the floors during cleaning, remove it as quickly as possible.

Equipment Selection

Foodservice equipment must meet certain standards if it will come in contact with food. NSF International is an organization that creates these national standards. NSF, whose logo is shown at left, is accredited by the American National Standards Institute (ANSI). NSF/ANSI standards for food equipment require that it be nonabsorbent, smooth, and corrosion resistant.

Food equipment must also be easy to clean, durable, and resistant to damage.

Installing and Maintaining Equipment

Stationary equipment should be easy to clean and easy to clean around. In the photo at left, the dishwasher is installed so that the floor can be cleaned easily.

When installing equipment, follow the manufacturer's recommendations. Also check with your regulatory authority for requirements. In general, stationary equipment should be installed as follows.

Floor-mounted equipment   Put floor-mounted equipment on legs at least six inches (15 centimeters) high, as shown in the photo below. Another option is to seal it to a masonry base.

Tabletop equipment   Put tabletop equipment on legs at least four inches (10 centimeters) high, as shown in the photo below. Or, seal it to the countertop.

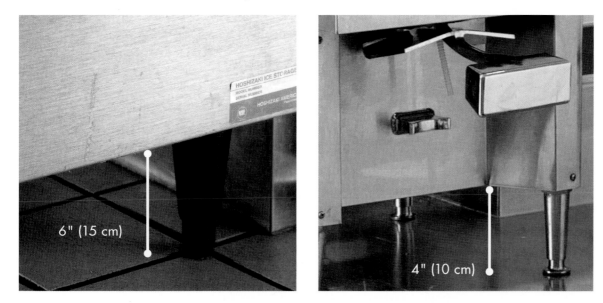

Once you have installed equipment, make sure it is maintained regularly by qualified people. Also, set up a maintenance schedule with your supplier or manufacturer. Check equipment regularly to be sure it is working correctly.

Dishwashing Machines

Dishwashers vary by size, style, and sanitizing method. For example, some sanitize with very hot water. Others use a chemical solution.

Consider these guidelines when selecting and installing dishwashers.

Installation   Dishwashers must be installed so that they are reachable and conveniently located. That installation must also keep utensils, equipment, and other food-contact surfaces from becoming contaminated. Always follow the manufacturer's instructions when installing, operating, and maintaining dishwashers.

Supplies   Use detergents and sanitizers approved by the local regulatory authority.

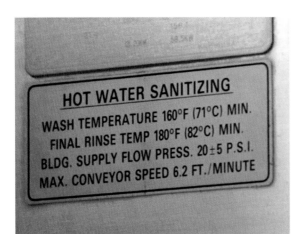

Settings   Purchase dishwashers that have the ability to measure the following:

- Water temperature
- Water pressure
- Cleaning and sanitizing chemical concentration

Information about the correct settings should be posted on the machine. The label in the photo at left shows an example.

Cleaning   Clean dishwashers as often as necessary. Follow the manufacturer's recommendations and local regulatory requirements.

Three-Compartment Sinks

Many operations use three-compartment sinks to clean and sanitize items manually in the operation. Purchase sinks that are large enough to accommodate large equipment and utensils. You should also have other methods for cleaning these large items, such as cleaning them in place.

Handwashing Stations

Handwashing stations should be put in areas that make it easy for staff to wash their hands often. Handwashing stations are required:

- In restrooms or directly next to them
- In areas used for food prep, service, and dishwashing

Handwashing sinks must be used only for handwashing and not for any other purpose. And, to prevent cross-contamination, make sure adequate barriers, as seen in the photo at left, are present on handwashing sinks, or that there is an adequate distance between handwashing sinks and food and food-contact surfaces so that water cannot splash on these items.

Make sure these stations work correctly and are well stocked and maintained. They must also be available at all times. This means that handwashing stations cannot be blocked by portable equipment or stacked full of dirty kitchenware. An example of this is shown in the photo at left.

See Table 9.1 for requirements at a handwashing station.

Table 9.1: **Requirements at a Handwashing Station**

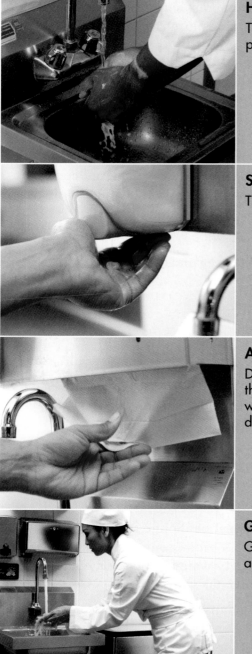

Hot- and cold-running water
The water must be drinkable and meet temperature and pressure requirements.

Soap
The soap can be liquid, bar, or powder.

A way to dry hands
Disposable paper towels or a continuous towel system that supplies the user with a clean towel can be used. Hands can also be dried with a hand dryer using either warm air or room-temperature air delivered at high velocity.

Garbage container
Garbage containers are required if disposable paper towels are used.

EMPLOYEES MUST WASH HANDS BEFORE RETURNING TO WORK

LOS EMPLEADOS DEBEN LAVARSE LAS MANOS ANTES DE VOLVER A TRABAJO

Signage
A clearly visible sign or poster must tell staff to wash hands before returning to work.

Utilities and Building Systems

An operation uses many utilities and building systems. Utilities include water, electricity, gas, sewage, and garbage disposal. Building systems include plumbing, lighting, and ventilation. There must be enough utilities to meet the needs of the operation. In addition, the utilities and systems must work correctly. If they do not, the risk of contamination is greater.

Water and Plumbing

There are national standards for water in the U.S. that are enforced by each regulatory authority. Only water that is drinkable can be used for the preparation of food and come in contact with food-contact surfaces. This is called potable water. This water may come from the following sources:

- Approved public water mains

- Private water sources that are regularly tested and maintained

- Closed, portable water containers

- Water transport vehicles

Regardless of where your water comes from, you should know how to prevent plumbing issues that can affect food safety.

If your operation has an on-site septic system, make sure it is properly tested and maintained.

Installation and maintenance   Plumbing that is not installed or maintained correctly can allow drinkable and unsafe water to be mixed. This can cause foodborne-illness outbreaks. Have only licensed plumbers work on the plumbing in your operation.

Cross-connection   The greatest challenge to water safety comes from cross-connections. A cross-connection is a physical link between safe water and dirty water, which can come from drains, sewers, or other wastewater sources.

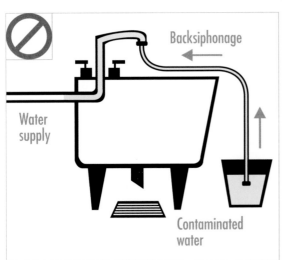

Water supply

Backsiphonage

Contaminated water

A cross-connection is dangerous because it can let backflow occur. Backflow is the reverse flow of contaminants through a cross-connection into a drinkable water supply. Backflow can be the result of pressure pushing contaminants back into the water supply. It can also happen when high water use in one area of an operation creates a vacuum in the plumbing system that sucks contaminants back into the water supply. This is called backsiphonage. A running faucet below the flood rim of a sink is an example of a cross-connection that can lead to backsiphonage. A running hose in a mop bucket is another example, as shown in the illustration at left.

Backflow prevention   The best way to prevent backflow is to avoid creating a cross-connection. Some ways to do this include:

- Do **NOT** attach a hose to a faucet unless a backflow prevention device is attached, such as a vacuum breaker. A vacuum breaker is a mechanical device that prevents backsiphonage, as seen in the photo at right. It does this by closing a check valve and sealing the water supply line shut when water flow is stopped.

- Other mechanical devices are used to prevent backflow. These include double check valves and reduced pressure zone backflow preventers. These devices include more than one check valve for sealing off the water supply. They also provide a way to determine if the check valves are operational.

Backflow prevention devices must be checked periodically to make sure they are working correctly. This must be done by a trained and certified technician. And the work must be documented. Always follow local requirements and manufacturers' recommendations.

The only sure way to prevent backflow is to create an air gap. An air gap is an air space that separates a water supply outlet from a potentially contaminated source. A sink that is correctly designed and installed usually has two air gaps, as shown in the graphic at right. One is between the faucet and the flood rim of the sink. The other is between the drainpipe of the sink and the floor drain of the operation.

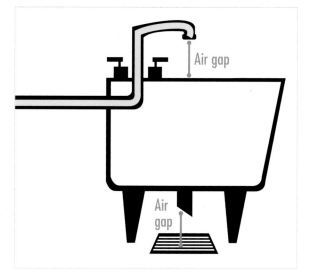

Grease condensation   A buildup of grease in pipes is another common problem in plumbing systems. Grease traps are often installed to prevent grease buildup from blocking the drain. If used, they should be put in by a licensed plumber and be easy to access. Also, make sure they are cleaned regularly following the manufacturer's recommendations. If the traps are not cleaned often enough or correctly, dirty water can back up. This backup could lead to odors and contamination.

Something to Think About

A popular catering company was shut down after multiple people got sick. The sink used to wash and clean vegetables was connected to the sewage drainpipe without backflow prevention. The company was not allowed to open until the issue was corrected.

Lighting

Good lighting makes it easier to clean things in your operation. It also provides a safer environment.

Lighting intensity—how bright the lights are in the operation—is usually measured in units called foot-candles or lux. Different areas of the facility have different lighting intensity requirements. Local jurisdictions usually require prep areas to be brighter than other areas. This allows staff to recognize the condition of food. It also allows staff to identify items that need cleaning.

Once the appropriate level of lighting has been installed in each area of the facility, you must monitor it. Replace any bulbs that have burned out. And make sure they are the correct size. All lights should have shatter-resistant lightbulbs or protective covers. These products prevent broken glass from contaminating food or food-contact surfaces.

Ventilation

Ventilation improves the air inside an operation. It removes heat, steam, and smoke from cooking lines. It also eliminates fumes and odors. If ventilation systems are not working correctly, grease and condensation will build up on walls and ceilings.

To prevent this, ventilation systems must be cleaned and maintained according to the manufacturer's recommendations.

Garbage

Garbage can attract pests and contaminate food, equipment, and utensils if not handled correctly. To control contamination from garbage, consider the following.

Garbage removal Garbage should be removed from prep areas as quickly as possible to prevent odors, pests, and possible contamination. Staff must be careful when removing garbage so they do not contaminate food or food-contact surfaces. The food handler in the photo at right has not been careful and may contaminate the prep table.

Cleaning of containers Clean the inside and outside of garbage containers frequently. This will help prevent the contamination of food and food-contact surfaces. It will also reduce odors and pests. Do not clean garbage containers near prep or food-storage areas.

Indoor containers Containers must be leakproof, waterproof, and pestproof. They also should be easy to clean. Containers must be covered when not in constant use. Women's restrooms must include a covered receptacle for sanitary napkins.

Designated storage areas Waste and recyclables must be stored separately from food and food-contact surfaces. The storage of these items must not create a nuisance or a public health hazard.

Outdoor containers Place garbage containers on a surface that is smooth, durable, and nonabsorbent. Asphalt and concrete are good choices, as shown in the photo at right. Make sure the containers have tight-fitting lids and are kept covered at all times. Keep their drain plugs in place.

Maintaining the Facility

Poor maintenance can cause food safety problems in your operation. To prevent problems, do the following:

- Clean the operation on a regular basis.

- Make sure all building systems work and are checked regularly.

- Make sure the building is sound. There should be no leaks, holes, or cracks in the floors, foundation, ceilings, or windows. In the photo at right, the maintenance worker is filling a crack in an exterior wall to keep pests out.

- Control pests.

- Maintain the outside of the building correctly, including patios and parking lots.

Apply Your Knowledge

What's Missing?   The handwashing station is missing 3 items. What are they?

① _____

② _____

③ _____

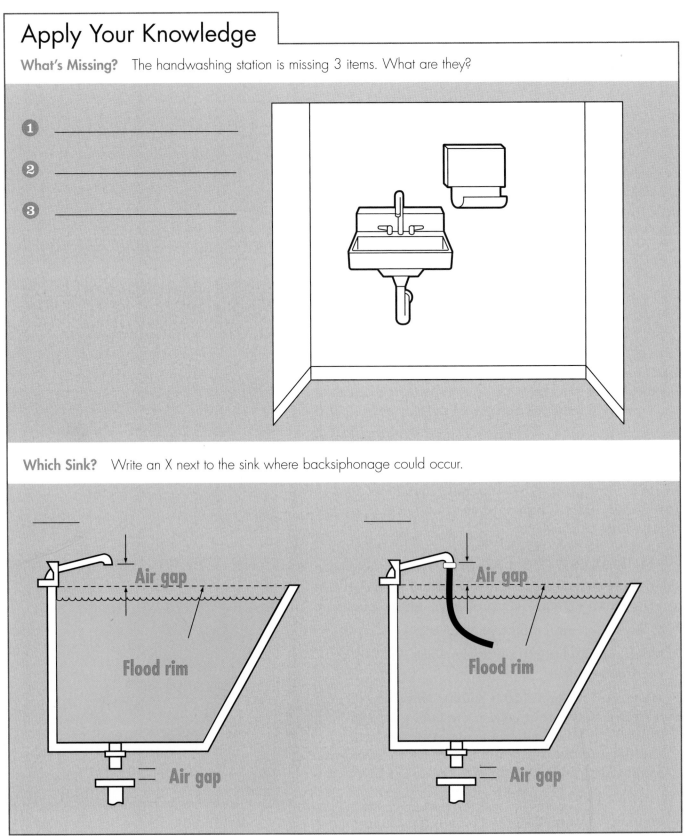

Which Sink?   Write an X next to the sink where backsiphonage could occur.

_____   _____

Air gap

Flood rim

Air gap

Air gap

Flood rim

Air gap

For answers, please turn to page 9.18.

Apply Your Knowledge

Garbage In, Garbage Out   Write an X next to each unsafe practice when handling garbage and garbage containers.

① _____ John cleans a garbage can on the floor drain grate, which is next to the grill.

② _____ Dave stacks garbage bags next to the prep table because he wants to take them out all at once.

③ _____ Steve sets garbage bags on the asphalt next to the dumpster and then throws each bag inside.

④ _____ Michelle throws empty cans into the recycling container, which is stored in the prep area.

⑤ _____ Tunya throws a burned hamburger into the open garbage can next to the sandwich line.

For answers, please turn to page 9.18.

Emergencies That Affect the Facility

Certain crises can affect the safety of the food you serve. Some of the most common include electrical power outages, fire, flooding, and sewage backups. These are considered by the local regulatory authority to be imminent health hazards. An imminent health hazard is a significant threat or danger to health that requires immediate correction or closure to prevent injury.

Other threats should also be considered.

Temperature control   Power failures and refrigeration breakdowns can threaten your ability to control the temperature of TCS food. This can result in the growth of pathogens.

Physical security   Unauthorized people inside a facility are a risk to food safety. This is especially true when they can access storage and processing areas. Also, acts of nature can weaken a facility's security, such as heavy storms.

Drinkable water supply   Threats to the drinkable water supply must also be considered. Broken water mains and breakdowns at water treatment facilities are a risk to the safety of food. Terrorist contamination of the water supply could also be a threat.

When faced with any of these crises, you must first determine if there is a significant risk to the safety or security of your food. If the risk is significant, service must be stopped. Then the local regulatory authority must be notified.

Spoiled or contaminated food must be thrown out, along with food in packaging that is not intact. Finally, you must decide how to correct the problem. This could include:

- Establishing time-temperature control of TCS food
- Cleaning and sanitizing surfaces in the operation
- Reestablishing the physical security of the operation
- Verifying that the water supply is drinkable

Regardless of how the problem is corrected, you will need approval from the local regulatory authority before continuing service.

Pest Management

Rodents, insects, and other pests are more than just unsightly to customers. They can damage food, supplies, and facilities. But the greatest danger comes from their ability to spread diseases, including foodborne illnesses.

Pest Prevention

Prevention is critical in pest control. Follow these three basic rules to keep your operation pest-free:

1 Deny pests access to the operation.

2 Deny pests food, water, and shelter.

3 Work with a licensed pest control operator (PCO).

Deny shelter   Careful cleaning eliminates the pests' food supply and destroys insect eggs. It also reduces the places pests can take shelter. Follow these guidelines to deny pests food and shelter:

- Throw out garbage quickly and correctly. Keep garbage containers clean and in good condition. Keep outdoor containers tightly covered. Clean up spills around garbage containers immediately, and wash containers regularly.

- Store recyclables in clean, pest-proof containers. Keep them as far away from your building as local regulations allow.

- Store all food and supplies correctly and as quickly as possible. Keep food and supplies away from walls and at least six inches (15 centimeters) off the floor. Use FIFO to rotate products, so that pests do not have time to settle into them and breed.

- Clean up food and beverage spills immediately, including crumbs and scraps.

Deny access   Pests can be brought inside with deliveries or through building openings. Follow these guidelines to prevent this:

- Check all deliveries before they enter your operation. Refuse shipments in which you find pests or signs of pests, as shown in the photo at right. This includes egg cases and body parts (legs, wings, etc.).

- Make sure all of the points where pests can access the building are secure. Screen all windows and vents, and patch or replace them when needed. Seal cracks in floors and walls and around pipes, as shown in the photo at right. Install self-closing doors and air curtains (also called air doors or fly fans) above or alongside doors.

Pest Control

Even after you have made every effort to keep pests out, they may still get into your operation. If this happens, you must work with a PCO to get them under control. Even if you only spot a few pests, they may actually be present in large numbers. This is an infestation and can be very difficult to eliminate. Pests leave signs, letting you know they are there. Look for live or dead insects or rodents, feces, nests, and damage on products, packaging, and the facility itself. An example of a rodent nest is shown in the photo at right. Contact your PCO immediately if you see these or any other pest-related problems, so that control measures can be taken. Poisonous or toxic pest-control materials should only be applied by a certified applicator.

Apply Your Knowledge

Keep 'Em Out!   Write an X next to each situation that can lead to a pest infestation.

1. _____ Food in the dry-storage room is stored against the wall and 6 inches off the floor.

2. _____ Air curtains are installed around the back door of a kitchen.

3. _____ Recyclables are stored overnight in a clean container in the kitchen.

4. _____ Food is rotated during storage so that the oldest products are used first.

5. _____ A dumpster is left open during the day to let it air out.

6. _____ A delivery driver brings a food delivery into the kitchen to be inspected.

7. _____ A food delivery is rejected because it contains packages with gnaw marks.

8. _____ The exterior of the operation has a three-inch hole.

For answers, please turn to page 9.18.

Study Questions

Circle the best answer to each question.

1 **What are the most important food safety features to look for when selecting flooring, wall, and ceiling materials?**

   A   Absorbent and durable

   B   Hard and durable

   C   Porous and durable

   D   Smooth and durable

2 **What organization creates national standards for foodservice equipment?**

   A   CDC

   B   EPA

   C   FDA

   D   NSF

3 **When installing tabletop equipment on legs, the space between the base of the equipment and the tabletop must be at least**

   A   2 inches (5 centimeters).

   B   4 inches (10 centimeters).

   C   6 inches (15 centimeters).

   D   8 inches (20 centimeters).

4 **An operation has a buildup of grease and condensation on the walls and ceiling. What is the most likely problem?**

   A   The ventilation system is not working correctly.

   B   The cleaning chemicals are not being used correctly.

   C   The staff are not cleaning the walls correctly.

   D   The grill is not being operated at a high-enough temperature.

5 **A handwashing station should have a garbage container, hot and cold water, signage, a way to dry hands, and**

   A   soap.

   B   a timer.

   C   a clock.

   D   gloves.

Study Questions

6   What is the only completely reliable method for preventing backflow?

  A   Air gap
  B   Ball valve
  C   Cross-connection
  D   Vacuum breaker

7   A food handler drops the end of a hose into a mop bucket and turns the water on to fill it. What has the food handler done wrong?

  A   Created a cross-connection
  B   Created an air-gap separation
  C   Prevented backflow
  D   Prevented atmospheric vacuuming

8   An operation received a violation in the outside area of the facility. The manager reviewed the area and saw that the dumpster was placed on a freshly graveled drive. The lids were closed, and the drain plug was in place to prevent the dumpster from draining. What was the problem?

  A   The dumpster lids should have been open to allow it to air out.
  B   The drain plug should have been removed to allow the dumpster to drain correctly.
  C   The surface underneath the dumpster should have been paved with concrete or asphalt.
  D   The dumpster should have been freshly painted so that food debris would not stick to surfaces.

9   A broken water main has caused the water in an operation to appear brown. What should the manager do?

  A   Boil the water for 1 minute before use.
  B   Contact the local regulatory authority before use.
  C   Use the water for everything except dishwashing.
  D   Use the water for everything except handwashing.

10   What is the best way to eliminate pests that have entered the operation?

  A   Raise the heat in the operation after-hours.
  B   Lower the heat in the operation after-hours.
  C   Work with a licensed pest control operator (PCO).
  D   Apply over-the-counter pesticides around the operation.

For answers, please turn to page 9.19.

Answers

9.10 What's Missing?

- Soap
- Sign stating that staff must wash hands before returning to work
- Garbage container for used paper towels

9.10 Which Sink?

Sink 2 should be marked.

9.11 Garbage In, Garbage Out

1, 2, and 4 should be marked.

9.13 Keep 'Em Out!

1, 3, 5, 6, and 8 should be marked.

9.15 Chapter Review Case Study

1 **What did Maria do right?**

- She had the burned-out lightbulbs replaced.
- She closed the door to prevent pests from entering the operation.

2 **What did Maria do wrong?**

Answers

- She should have rejected the delivery. The gnawed food items and insect wings are signs of pests.

- She should have had the garbage removed from the back door; this can attract pests.

- She should have placed a garbage container near the handwashing station.

- She should not have ignored the brown liquid by the floor drain. She should determine if it is a risk to food safety.

9.16   Study Questions

1 D

2 D

3 B

4 A

5 A

6 A

7 A

8 C

9 B

10 C

Cleaning and Sanitizing

Food can easily be contaminated if you do not keep your facility and equipment clean and sanitized. Cleaning removes food and other dirt from a surface. Sanitizing reduces pathogens on a surface to safe levels.

Cleaners

Cleaners must be stable, noncorrosive, and safe to use. There are a variety of cleaners available, each with a different purpose. These include:

- Detergents
- Degreasers
- Delimers
- Abrasive cleaners

Ask your supplier to help you pick cleaners that meet your needs. To use cleaners correctly, follow these guidelines:

- Follow manufacturers' instructions carefully, as the manager in the photo at left is doing. If not used the correct way, cleaners may not work and can even be dangerous.
- Only use cleaners for their intended purpose. **NEVER** use one type of cleaner in place of another unless the intended use is the same.

Sanitizers

Food-contact surfaces must be sanitized after they have been cleaned and rinsed. This can be done by using heat or chemicals.

Heat Sanitizing

One way to sanitize items is to soak them in hot water. For this method to work, the water must be at least 171°F (77°C). The items must be soaked for at least 30 seconds. Another way to sanitize items with heat is to run them through a high-temperature dishwasher.

Chemical Sanitizing

Tableware, utensils, and equipment can be sanitized by soaking them in a chemical sanitizing solution. Or you can rinse, swab, or spray them with sanitizing solution, as shown in the photo at left.

Three common types of chemical sanitizers are chlorine, iodine, and quaternary ammonium compounds, or quats. Chemical sanitizers are regulated by state and federal environmental protection agencies.

In some cases, you can use detergent-sanitizer blends to sanitize. Operations that have two-compartment sinks often use these. If you use a detergent-sanitizer blend, use it once to clean. Then use it a second time to sanitize.

Sanitizer Effectiveness

Several factors influence the effectiveness of chemical sanitizers. The most critical include concentration, temperature, contact time, water hardness, and pH.

Concentration   Sanitizer solution is a mix of chemical sanitizer and water. The concentration of this mix—the amount of sanitizer to water—is critical. Too little sanitizer may make the solution weak and useless. Too much sanitizer may make the solution too strong and unsafe. It can also leave a bad taste on items or corrode metal.

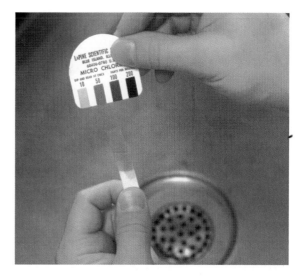

Concentration is measured in parts per million (ppm). To check the concentration of a sanitizer solution, use a test kit, as shown in the photo at right. Make sure it is made for the sanitizer being used. These kits are usually available from the chemical manufacturer or supplier. Make sure they are available at all times and easily accessible to employees.

Hard water, food bits, and leftover detergent can reduce the solution's effectiveness. Change the solution when it looks dirty or its concentration is too low. Check the concentration often.

Temperature   The water in sanitizing solution must be the correct temperature. Follow manufacturers' recommendations.

Contact time   For a sanitizer solution to kill pathogens, it must make contact with the object being sanitized for a specific amount of time. This is called contact time. For example, the bain in the photo at right is being sanitized in an iodine sanitizing solution. The bain must be in contact with the solution for at least 30 seconds.

Water hardness   Water hardness can affect how well a sanitizer works. Water hardness is determined by the amount of minerals in your water. Find out what your water hardness is from your municipality. Then work with your supplier to identify the correct amount of sanitizer to use for your water.

pH   Water pH can also affect a sanitizer. Find out what the pH of your water is from your municipality. Then work with your supplier to find out the correct amount of sanitizer to use for your water.

Table 10.1 summarizes some guidelines for using different types of sanitizers.

Table 10.1: General Guidelines for the Effective Use of Chlorine, Iodine, and Quats

	Chlorine		Iodine	Quats
Water temperature	≥100°F (38°C)	≥75°F (24°C)	68°F (20°C)	75°F (24°C)
Water pH	≤10	≤8	≤5 or as per manufacturer's recommendation	As per manufacturer's recommendation
Water hardness	As per manufacturer's recommendation		As per manufacturer's recommendation	≤500 ppm or as per manufacturer's recommendation
Sanitizer concentration	50–99 ppm	50–99 ppm	12.5–25 ppm	As per manufacturer's recommendation
Sanitizer contact time	≥7 seconds	≥7 seconds	≥30 seconds	≥30 seconds

How and When to Clean and Sanitize

Surfaces that do not touch food only need to be cleaned and rinsed to prevent the accumulation of dirt. However, any surface that touches food must be cleaned, rinsed, and sanitized.

Cleaning and Sanitizing Surfaces

To clean and sanitize a surface, follow the steps detailed here. If surfaces have not been cleaned and sanitized properly, take corrective action immediately.

1 Scrape or remove food bits from the surface.

- Use the correct cleaning tool, such as a nylon brush or pad, or a cloth towel.

2 Wash the surface.

- Prepare the cleaning solution with an approved cleaner.
- Wash the surface with the correct cleaning tool, such as a cloth towel.

3 Rinse the surface.

- Use clean water.
- Rinse the surface with the correct cleaning tool, such as a cloth towel.

4 Sanitize the surface.

- Use the correct sanitizing solution.
- Prepare the concentration per manufacturer requirements.
- Use the correct tool, such as a cloth towel, to sanitize the surface.
- Make sure the entire surface has come in contact with the sanitizing solution.

5 Allow the surface to air-dry.

When to Clean and Sanitize

All food-contact surfaces need to be cleaned and sanitized at these times:

- After they are used
- Before working with a different type of food, for example between prepping raw chicken and cutting lettuce
- After handling different raw TCS fruits and vegetables, for example between cutting melons and leafy greens
- Any time there is an interruption during a task and the items being used may have been contaminated
- After four hours if items are in constant use

Cleaning and Sanitizing Stationary Equipment

Equipment manufacturers will usually provide instructions for cleaning and sanitizing stationary equipment, such as a slicer. In general, follow these steps:

- Unplug the equipment.
- Take the removable parts off the equipment. Wash, rinse, and sanitize them by hand. You can also run the parts through a dishwasher if allowed.
- Scrape or remove food from the equipment surfaces.

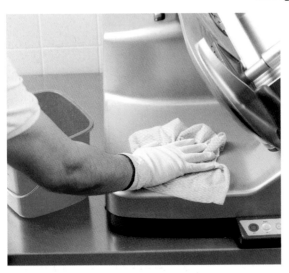

- Wash the equipment surfaces. Use a cleaning solution prepared with an approved cleaner. Wash the equipment with the correct cleaning tool, such as a nylon brush or pad, or a cloth towel.
- Rinse the equipment surfaces with clean water. Use a cloth towel or other correct tool.
- Sanitize the equipment surfaces as the food handler in the photo at left is doing. Make sure the sanitizer comes in contact with each surface. The concentration of the sanitizer must meet requirements.
- Allow all surfaces to air-dry. Put the unit back together.

Something to Think About

Deli slicers pose a risk of cross-contamination if not cleaned and sanitized properly. They can be a source of listeriosis, a pathogen that is often linked to deli meats and cheeses and that can cause a foodborne illness. This is why it is important to clean and sanitize slicers every four hours.

Clean-in-Place Equipment

Some pieces of equipment, such as soft-serve yogurt machines, are designed to have cleaning and sanitizing solutions pumped through them. Because many of them hold and dispense TCS food, they must be cleaned and sanitized every day unless otherwise indicated by the manufacturer.

Apply Your Knowledge

Was It Sanitized? Circle the correct answer for each question. For all situations, assume water hardness and pH are at the correct level.

1. Jack mixed a quat sanitizer with 75°F (24°C) water. A test kit showed the concentration was correct according to the manufacturer's recommendations. He soaked some utensils in the solution for 30 seconds. Were the utensils sanitized correctly? **Yes   No**

2. Josh mixed a chlorine sanitizer with 75°F (24°C) water. A test kit showed the concentration was 25 ppm. He soaked some plates in the solution for 7 seconds. Was the tableware sanitized correctly? **Yes   No**

3. Cecelia mixed an iodine sanitizer with 68°F (20°C) water. A test kit showed the concentration was 8 ppm. She put a hotel pan in the solution for 30 seconds. Was the hotel pan sanitized correctly? **Yes   No**

4. Jarmin mixed a chlorine sanitizer with 100°F (38°C) water. A test kit showed the concentration was 50 ppm. She put a mixing bowl in the solution for 7 seconds. Was the mixing bowl sanitized correctly? **Yes   No**

5. Marc filled a sink with 165°F (74°C) water. He put the slicer parts in the hot water to soak for 30 seconds. Were the slicer parts sanitized correctly? **Yes   No**

For answers, please turn to page 10.24.

Apply Your Knowledge

Take the Correct Steps   Put the steps for cleaning and sanitizing in order by writing the number of the step in the space provided.

A. _____   Sanitize the surface.

B. _____   Wash the surface.

C. _____   Allow the surface to air-dry.

D. _____   Rinse the surface.

E. _____   Remove food from the surface.

To Sanitize or Not to Sanitize   Write an X next to each situation that requires the food handler to clean and sanitize the item being used.

1 _____   Jorge has used the same knife to shuck oysters for 2 hours.

2 _____   Bill has finished deboning chicken and wants to use the same cutting board to fillet fish.

3 _____   Kristen has returned to the slicer to continue slicing cheese after being called away to help with the lunch rush.

4 _____   Amanda has been slicing turkey on the same slicer from 8:00 a.m. to 12:00 p.m.

For answers, please turn to page 10.24.

Dishwashing

Tableware and utensils are often cleaned and sanitized in a dishwashing machine. Larger items such as pots and pans are often cleaned by hand in a three-compartment sink. Whichever method you use, you must follow specific practices so items are cleaned and sanitized. Then you must make sure you store the items so they do not become contaminated.

Machine Dishwashing

Dishwashing machines sanitize by using either hot water or a chemical sanitizing solution.

High-Temperature Machines

High-temperature machines use hot water to clean and sanitize. If the water is not hot enough, items will not be sanitized. Extremely hot water can also bake food onto the items.

The temperature of the final sanitizing rinse must be at least 180°F (82°C), as shown in the photo at right. For stationary-rack, single-temperature machines, it must be at least 165°F (74°C). The dishwasher must have a built-in thermometer that checks water temperature at the manifold. This is where the water sprays into the tank.

Chemical-Sanitizing Machines

Chemical-sanitizing machines can clean and sanitize items at much lower temperatures. Follow the dishwasher manufacturer's guidelines.

Dishwasher Operation

Operate your dishwasher according to the manufacturer's recommendations, and keep it in good repair. However, no matter what type of machine you use, you should follow these guidelines.

Keeping the machine clean   Clean the machine as often as needed, checking it at least once a day. Clear spray nozzles of food and foreign objects. Remove mineral deposits when needed. Fill tanks with clean water, and make sure detergent and sanitizer dispensers are filled.

Preparing items for cleaning   Scrape items before washing them. If necessary, items can be rinsed or presoaked. This may be necessary when handling items with dried-on food.

Loading dish racks   Use the correct dish racks. Load them so the water spray will reach all surfaces, as shown in the photo at (top) left. **NEVER** overload dish racks.

Drying items   Air-dry all items. **NEVER** use a towel to dry items. Doing this could contaminate the items. Make sure they are completely dry before stacking or storing them.

Monitoring   Check water temperature, pressure, and sanitizer levels. Take appropriate corrective action if necessary.

Operations using high-temperature dishwashing machines must provide staff with an easy and quick way to measure the surface temperatures of items being sanitized. The method used must provide an irreversible record of the highest temperature reached during the sanitizing rinse. This ensures that the dishwasher can reach correct sanitizing temperatures during operation. Maximum registering thermometers, as shown in the picture at (middle) left, or heat-sensitive tape are good tools for checking temperatures.

Manual Dishwashing

Operations often use a three-compartment sink to clean and sanitize large items.

Preparing a Three-Compartment Sink

The sink must be set up correctly before use, as shown in the photo at (bottom) left.

- Clean and sanitize each sink and drain board.

- Fill the first sink with detergent and water. The water temperature must be at least 110°F (43°C). Follow the manufacturer's recommendations.

- Fill the second sink with clean water. This is not necessary if items will be spray-rinsed instead of being dipped.

- Fill the third sink with water and sanitizer to the correct concentration. Hot water can be used as an alternative. Follow the guidelines on pages 10.2 through 10.4 and the manufacturer's recommendations.

- Provide a clock with a second hand. This will let food handlers time how long items have been in the sanitizer.

Cleaning and Sanitizing in a Three-Compartment Sink

Follow these steps to clean and sanitize items in a three-compartment sink.

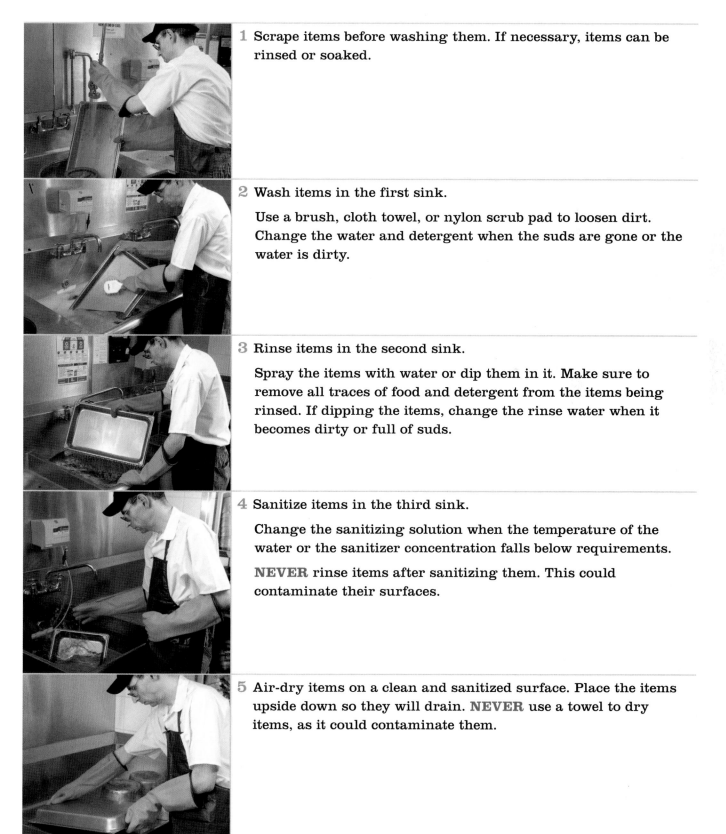

1 Scrape items before washing them. If necessary, items can be rinsed or soaked.

2 Wash items in the first sink.

Use a brush, cloth towel, or nylon scrub pad to loosen dirt. Change the water and detergent when the suds are gone or the water is dirty.

3 Rinse items in the second sink.

Spray the items with water or dip them in it. Make sure to remove all traces of food and detergent from the items being rinsed. If dipping the items, change the rinse water when it becomes dirty or full of suds.

4 Sanitize items in the third sink.

Change the sanitizing solution when the temperature of the water or the sanitizer concentration falls below requirements.

NEVER rinse items after sanitizing them. This could contaminate their surfaces.

5 Air-dry items on a clean and sanitized surface. Place the items upside down so they will drain. **NEVER** use a towel to dry items, as it could contaminate them.

Storing Tableware and Equipment

Once utensils, tableware, and equipment have been cleaned and sanitized, they must be stored in a way that will protect them from contamination. Follow these guidelines.

Storage   Store tableware and utensils at least six inches (15 centimeters) off the floor. Protect them from dirt and moisture.

Storage surfaces   Clean and sanitize drawers and shelves before storing clean items.

Glasses and flatware   Store glasses and cups upside down on a clean and sanitized shelf or rack. Store flatware and utensils with handles up, as shown in the photo at left. Staff can then pick them up without touching food-contact surfaces, which will help prevent the transfer of pathogens such as Norovirus.

Trays and carts   Clean and sanitize trays and carts used to carry clean tableware and utensils. Check them daily, and clean as often as needed.

Stationary equipment   Keep the food-contact surfaces of stationary equipment covered until ready for use.

Apply Your Knowledge

The New Dishwasher   List the missing or wrong steps in the story below.

Chris started work just as the breakfast rush had begun. A load of dirty dishes had just been put into the new dishwasher. There already were a lot of pots and pans to wash in the three-compartment sink, so Chris quickly got started. He scraped the dishes into a garbage container and stacked them on the drain board next to the first sink compartment. Then he filled the first compartment with hot water and added dish detergent. He put several pans in the soapy water to soak.

Next, Chris filled the remaining two compartments with warm water. He added iodine sanitizer to the third compartment. He used a thermometer to check the water temperature and then a test kit to check the sanitizer concentration. Both were good.

Using a nylon scrub pad, Chris worked on the pans until they were clean. As he finished each one, he dipped it in the sanitizing solution. Because customers had complained of an iodine flavor on tableware, Chris wanted to make sure there was no sanitizer left on the pans. As he pulled each pan out of the sanitizer, he placed it into the rinse water to soak for a few seconds. Then he put it on the clean drain board to air-dry.

What did Chris do wrong?

_____

_____

_____

For answers, please turn to page 10.24.

Apply Your Knowledge

Sarah's Dilemma   List the missing or wrong steps in the story below.

Sarah noticed that the dirty dishes had started to pile up. She quickly unloaded the dishwashing machine and got a dish cart for the clean dishes. Sarah saw a few crumbs on the cart. To clean it, she dipped a cloth towel in the dishwater in her three-compartment sink and wiped off the crumbs.

In the meantime, the carts of dirty dishes had grown. Sarah quickly loaded a dish rack with as many dishes as she could fit into it. She glanced into the dishwasher before pushing in the rack. She noticed a heavy buildup of mineral deposits on the spray arm and inside the compartment. She closed the door and started the dishwasher.

What did Sarah do wrong?

_____

_____

_____

_____

_____

What's Wrong with This Picture?   There are several things wrong with this three-compartment sink. Identify as many as you can in the space provided.

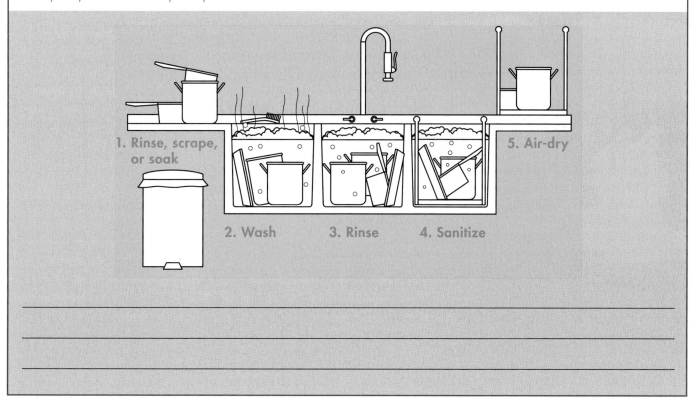

1. Rinse, scrape, or soak
2. Wash
3. Rinse
4. Sanitize
5. Air-dry

_____

_____

_____

For answers, please turn to page 10.24.

Cleaning and Sanitizing in the Operation

Keeping your operation clean means using the correct tools, supplies, and storage to prevent contamination. Many of the chemicals you will use are hazardous, so you also have to know how to handle them to prevent injury.

For all of your cleaning efforts to come together, you need a master cleaning schedule. Making this schedule work also means training and monitoring your staff to be sure they can follow it.

Wiping Cloths

Wiping cloths are often used in operations to wipe up food spills and to wipe down equipment surfaces. There are two types of wiping cloths used in operations—wet cloths and dry cloths. Each has its own requirements. **NEVER** use cloths that are meant for wiping food spills for any other purpose.

Wet cloths   Store wet wiping cloths used for wiping counters and other equipment surfaces in a sanitizer solution between uses, as shown in the photo at left. Change the solution when it no longer meets requirements for the sanitizer being used. Always keep cloths that come in contact with raw meat, fish, and poultry separate from other cleaning cloths.

Dry cloths   Wiping cloths that will be used to wipe food spills from tableware, such as from a plate during service, must be kept dry while in use. The photo at left shows a dry wiping cloth being used for this purpose. These cloths must **NOT** contain food debris or be visibly dirty during use.

Cleaning the Premises

Many surfaces in the operation do not normally come in contact with food. These are called nonfood-contact surfaces. Examples include floors, walls, ceilings, and equipment exteriors. Because they are not food-contact surfaces, they do not need to be sanitized. However, they do need to be cleaned regularly. This prevents dust, dirt, and food residue from building up. Not only will this prevent the growth of pathogens, but it will also prevent pests.

Cleaning up after People Who Get Sick

If vomit or diarrhea contacts surfaces in the operation, it must be cleaned up correctly. These substances can carry Norovirus, which is very contagious. Cleaning these surfaces correctly can prevent food from becoming contaminated. It will also keep others from becoming sick.

To be effective, operations must have procedures for cleaning up vomit and diarrhea. These procedures must address specific actions that employees must take to minimize contamination and exposure to food, surfaces, and people. It is critical that employees be trained on these procedures.

Using and Storing Cleaning Tools and Supplies

Your staff needs many tools and supplies to keep the operation clean. However, these items can contaminate food and surfaces if they are not used and stored correctly.

Storing Cleaning Tools and Supplies

Cleaning tools must be stored so that they do not contaminate food and equipment. It is a best practice to store these items in a designated area away from food. Cleaning tools should also be stored in a way that makes it easy to clean the area they are stored in. The storage area should have the following:

- Good lighting so staff can see chemicals easily
- Hooks for hanging mops, brooms, and other cleaning tools
- Utility sink for filling buckets and washing cleaning tools
- Floor drain for dumping dirty water, as shown in the photo at right

To prevent contamination, **NEVER** clean mops, brushes, or other tools in sinks used for handwashing, food prep, or dishwashing. Additionally, **NEVER** dump mop water or other liquid waste into toilets or urinals.

When storing cleaning tools, consider the following:

- Place mops in a position to air-dry without soiling walls, equipment, or supplies.
- Clean and rinse buckets. Let them air-dry, and then store them with other tools.

If chemicals or cleaning tools have not been used or stored correctly, take corrective action immediately.

Using Foodservice Chemicals

Many of the chemicals used in an operation can be hazardous, especially if they are used or stored the wrong way. One of the biggest dangers is cross-contamination. To reduce your risk, follow these guidelines.

Use   Only chemicals approved for use in a foodservice operation should be used. **NEVER** keep chemicals that are not required to operate or maintain the establishment. To prevent contamination, always cover or remove items that could become contaminated before using chemicals. After using chemicals, make sure to clean and sanitize equipment and utensils. Always follow the law and manufacturers' directions when using chemicals.

Storage   Chemicals must be stored in their original containers. Some operations also designate specific areas for storing chemicals. Whether or not this is done, chemicals must be kept separate from food, equipment, utensils, and linens. This separation can be done either of these ways:

- By spacing chemicals apart from other items
- By partitioning off chemicals from other items stored in the same area

Regardless of the method used, chemicals must always be stored below food, equipment, utensils, and linens.

Labels   Chemicals stored in their original container should have a manufacturer's label. That label must include the directions for use and be clear enough to read. If chemicals are transferred to a new working container, the label on that container must list the common name of the chemical. The photo at left shows a working container labeled with the common name of the chemical.

Developing a Cleaning Program

To develop an effective cleaning program for your operation, you must focus on three things:

- Creating a master cleaning schedule
- Training your staff to follow it
- Monitoring the program to make sure it works

Creating a Master Cleaning Schedule

Create a master cleaning schedule with the following information.

What should be cleaned List all cleaning jobs in one area, or list jobs in the order they should be performed. Include both food and nonfood surfaces as items that need to be cleaned.

Who should clean it Assign each task to a specific individual.

When it should be cleaned Staff should clean and sanitize as needed. Schedule major cleaning when food will not be contaminated or service will not be affected. Schedule work shifts to allow enough time.

How it should be cleaned Have clear, written procedures for cleaning. List cleaning tools and chemicals by name. Post cleaning instructions near the item. Always follow manufacturers' instructions when cleaning equipment.

Training Your Staff to Follow the Program

Schedule time for training. Work with small groups or conduct training by area, as shown in the photo at right.

Monitoring the Cleaning Program

Make sure the cleaning program is working.

- Supervise daily cleaning routines.
- Check all cleaning tasks against the master schedule every day.
- Change the master schedule as needed for any changes in menu, procedures, or equipment.
- Ask staff during meetings for input on the program.

Apply Your Knowledge

Was It Done Correctly? Write an X next to the situation if the food handler used or stored the cleaning tool or chemical the wrong way.

1 _____ Gail was in a rush to put a delivery away. She placed the cleaning chemicals on the top shelf of the shelving rack above the canned goods.

2 _____ Raul filled three spray bottles with sanitizer. Since the chemical looked red, he did not label the spray bottles.

3 _____ Jasmina was about to take a plate out to a table and she noticed some drips on the edge of the plate. She grabbed a clean, dry cloth and wiped off the plate.

4 _____ Sasha emptied a bucket of dirty mop water into the floor drain. He rinsed the mop and hung it to dry. Then he cleaned and rinsed the bucket.

5 _____ Laura washed, rinsed, and sanitized a table by spraying it with sanitizer and allowing it to air dry. She then placed the bottle of sanitizer on the prep table.

6 _____ Andy used a chemical cleaner on the dishwashing machine. The sprayer on the bottle stopped working when it was only half empty, so he threw it in the garbage.

What's Wrong with This Picture? There are many things wrong with this storage area. Identify as many as you can in the space provided.

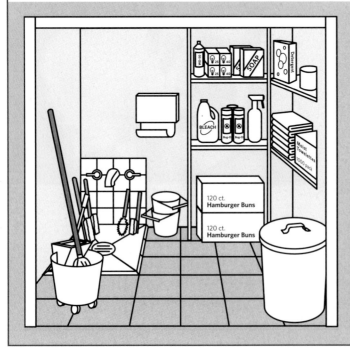

_____

_____

_____

_____

_____

_____

_____

_____

_____

For answers, please turn to page 10.25.

Chapter Summary

- Cleaning removes food and other dirt from a surface. Sanitizing reduces the number of pathogens on a surface to safe levels. You must clean and rinse a surface before it can be sanitized. Then the surface must be allowed to air-dry. Surfaces can be sanitized with hot water or a chemical sanitizing solution. Each sanitizing method and sanitizer chemical has specific requirements for use.

- All surfaces should be cleaned and rinsed. Food-contact surfaces must be cleaned and sanitized after every use. You should also clean and sanitize each time you begin working with a different type of food or after handling different, raw TCS fruits and vegetables. Also clean and sanitize surfaces when a task is interrupted. If items are in constant use, they must be cleaned and sanitized every four hours.

- To clean and sanitize a surface, first remove any food from the surface. Then wash and rinse the surface. Finally, sanitize the surface, and let it air-dry.

- Tableware and utensils can be washed in dishwashers or by hand in a three-compartment sink. Always follow manufacturers' instructions when using dishwashers. Make sure your machine is clean and in good working condition. Check the temperature and pressure of wash and rinse cycles daily.

- Before washing items in a three-compartment sink, clean and sanitize the sinks and drain boards. Scrape, rinse, or presoak items before washing them. Then wash them in a detergent solution, and rinse them in clean water. Next, sanitize them for a specific amount of time in either hot water or a chemical sanitizing solution. Finally, they should be air-dried. Once cleaned and sanitized, tableware and equipment should be protected from contamination.

- Wet and dry wiping cloths may be used to wipe up food spills and wipe down equipment surfaces. Wet cloths may be used for wiping equipment surfaces. They should be stored in a sanitizer solution between uses. Clean, dry wiping cloths may be used to wipe food spills from tableware.

- Operations must have procedures for cleaning up vomit and diarrhea. Make sure employees are trained on these procedures and know what to do.

- Chemicals can contaminate food and equipment if the chemicals are not used or stored correctly. Use only chemicals approved for use in foodservice operations. Before using chemicals, cover or remove items to prevent them from being contaminated. Clean and sanitize equipment and utensils after using chemicals.

- Make sure chemicals are clearly labeled. Store cleaning supplies and tools away from food and equipment.

- Create a master cleaning schedule listing all cleaning tasks. Train staff to follow it. Monitor the cleaning program to keep it effective and supervise cleaning procedures. Make adjustments as needed.

Chapter Review Case Study

Keeping an operation clean and sanitized involves using the correct tools and products for a cleaning job; cleaning and sanitizing items the correct way at the right time; storing items so they remain safe to use; handling chemicals the correct way; and developing and following a cleaning program.

Now, take what you have learned in this chapter and apply it to the following case study.

Andy was just hired as the new general manager at the Twin Trees Family Restaurant. One of his first projects was to create a new cleaning program. He started by taking a walk through the operation. His first stop was the storage area for cleaning tools and supplies. It had a utility sink and a floor drain, but the hot water in the sink was not working. He also noticed two sets of mops and brooms stored on the floor. The storage area was small, but it was well organized and well lit. All the containers were clearly labeled.

1 **Should Andy suggest any changes to the storage room, tools, or chemicals?**

   Yes   No   **If yes, what changes should he suggest?**

   _____

   _____

   _____

   _____

   _____

   _____

   _____

   _____

   _____

   _____

   _____

Chapter Review Case Study

Next, Andy watched Clara, a new prep cook, to see how she cleaned and sanitized her areas. Clara cut some melons on a cutting board. Then she wiped it down with a cloth towel. Clara put the cloth towel in a bucket of sanitizing solution to soak while she chopped some fresh spinach. Using the same cloth towel, she wiped down the board after she finished the spinach. Then, she butterflied some pork chops on the same board. Afterward, Clara wiped the board a third time with the same cloth towel.

2 **Did Clara do anything wrong?**

Yes   No   **If yes, what changes should Andy suggest?**

_____

_____

_____

_____

_____

_____

Andy also watched many other staff members perform cleaning and sanitizing tasks that week. With the help of some senior staff, Andy created a master cleaning schedule.

3 **What steps should Andy take to make sure everyone follows the master cleaning schedule?**

_____

_____

_____

_____

_____

_____

_____

For answers, please turn to page 10.25.

Study Questions

Circle the best answer to each question.

1 **What is required for measuring the sanitizing rinse temperature in a high-temperature dishwashing machine?**

   A Infrared thermometer

   B Time-temperature indicator

   C Maximum registering thermometer

   D Thermocouple with immersion probe

2 **What is the acceptable contact time when sanitizing food-contact surfaces?**

   A Soak the item in very hot water for 7 seconds.

   B Soak the item in an iodine solution for 7 seconds.

   C Soak the item in a chlorine solution for 7 seconds.

   D Soak the item in an ammonia solution for 7 seconds.

3 **If food-contact surfaces are in constant use, how often must they be cleaned and sanitized?**

   A Every 4 hours

   B Every 5 hours

   C Every 6 hours

   D Every 7 hours

4 **What must food handlers do to make sure sanitizing solution for use on food-contact surfaces has been made correctly?**

   A Test the solution with a sanitizer kit.

   B Use very hot water when making the solution.

   C Try out the solution on a food-contact surface.

   D Mix the solution with equal parts of water.

5 **George is getting ready to wash dishes in a three-compartment sink. What should be his first task?**

   A Remove leftover food from the dishes.

   B Fill the first sink with detergent and water.

   C Clean and sanitize the sinks and drain boards.

   D Make sure there is a working clock with a second hand.

Study Questions

6 **Which feature is most important for a chemical storage area?**

A Good lighting

B Single-use towels

C Nonskid floor mats

D Emergency shower system

7 **How should flatware and utensils that have been cleaned and sanitized be stored?**

A With handles facing up

B Below cleaning supplies

C Four inches (10 centimeters) from the floor

D In drawers that have been washed and rinsed

8 **What is the correct way to clean and sanitize a prep table?**

A Remove food from the surface, sanitize, rinse, wash, air-dry

B Remove food from the surface, wash, rinse, sanitize, air-dry

C Remove food from the surface, wash, sanitize, air-dry, rinse

D Remove food from the surface, air-dry, wash, rinse, sanitize

9 **Pete the buser poured some cleaner from its original container into a smaller, working container. What else does he need to do?**

A Label the working container with its contents

B Read the safety data sheet (SDS) for the cleaner

C Use a new wiping cloth when first using the working container

D Note on the original container that some cleaner was put into a working container

10 **What information should a master cleaning schedule contain?**

A What should be cleaned, and when

B What should be cleaned, when, and by whom

C What should be cleaned, when, by whom, and how

D What should be cleaned, when, by whom, how, and why

For answers, please turn to page 10.25.

Answers

10.7 Was It Sanitized?

1 Yes

2 No

3 No

4 Yes

5 No

10.8 Take the Correct Steps

4, 2, 5, 3, 1

10.8 To Sanitize or Not to Sanitize

2, 3, and 4 should be marked.

10.12 The New Dishwasher

Here is what Chris did wrong:

- He did not clean and sanitize the sink compartments and drain boards before starting.

- He did not check the water temperature in the first sink compartment.

- He did not rinse the items before sanitizing them. He rinsed the items after sanitizing, which could contaminate them.

- He did not time how long the pots and pans were in the sanitizer.

10.13 Sarah's Dilemma

Here is what Sarah did wrong:

- She did not clean and sanitize the cart for clean tableware.

- She did not rinse, scrape, or soak the dirty dishes before putting them into the dish rack.

- She overloaded the dish rack.

- She did not clean the heavy mineral deposits from the machine before starting the day.

10.13 What's Wrong with This Picture?

- Soap suds from the wash compartment have been carried over into the rinse compartment.

- There is no clock with a second hand. Staff would not be able to time how long an item has been immersed in the sanitizer.

- A cleaned and sanitized pot is not being air-dried correctly. It should be upside down.

Answers

10.18   Was It Done Correctly?

1, 2, 5, and 6 should be marked.

10.18   What's Wrong with This Picture?

- There are no hooks for the brushes and mop to air-dry.
- The chemical spray bottle is not labeled.
- Food is being stored in the area.

10.20   Chapter Review Case Study

1 Yes. Andy should have the hot water fixed. He also should have hooks installed to hang up the mops and brooms.

2 Yes. Clara should have washed, rinsed, and sanitized the cutting board at these times:
  - Before cutting the melons
  - After cutting the melons and before chopping the spinach
  - After chopping the spinach and before butterflying the pork chops
  - After butterflying the pork chops

3 For Andy's cleaning program to work, he should do the following:
  - Train the staff on the cleaning and sanitizing tasks.
  - Supervise daily cleaning routines.
  - Check all cleaning tasks against the master cleaning schedule daily.
  - Change the master schedule as needed for any changes in the menu, procedures, or equipment.
  - Ask staff during meetings for input on the program.

10.22   Study Questions

1	C	6	A
2	C	7	A
3	A	8	B
4	A	9	A
5	C	10	C

Organisms That Cause Foodborne Illness

Bacteria

Bacteria	*Bacillus cereus (ba-SIL-us SEER-ee-us)*
Illness	*Bacillus cereus* gastroenteritis *(ba-SIL-us SEER-ee-us GAS-tro-EN-ter-I-tiss)*

Bacillus cereus is a spore-forming bacteria found in dirt. It can produce two different toxins when allowed to grow to high levels. The toxins cause different illnesses.

Food Commonly Linked with the Bacteria	Most Common Symptoms	Prevention Measures
Diarrhea illness • Cooked vegetables • Meat products • Milk Vomiting illness • Cooked rice dishes, including fried rice and rice pudding	Diarrhea illness • Watery diarrhea • No vomiting Vomiting illness • Nausea • Vomiting	• Cook food to minimum internal temperatures. • Hold food at the correct temperatures. • Cool food correctly. • Control time and temperature.

Bacteria	*Listeria monocytogenes (liss-TEER-ee-uh MON-o-SI-TAHJ-uh-neez)*
Illness	Listeriosis *(liss-TEER-ee-O-sis)*

Listeria monocytogenes is found in dirt, water, and plants. Unlike other bacteria, it grows in cool, moist environments. The illness is uncommon in healthy people, but high-risk populations are especially vulnerable—particularly pregnant women.

Food Commonly Linked with the Bacteria	Most Common Symptoms	Prevention Measures
• Raw meat • Unpasteurized dairy products • Ready-to-eat food, such as deli meat, hot dogs, and soft cheeses	Pregnant women • Miscarriage Newborns • Sepsis • Pneumonia • Meningitis	• Throw out any product that has passed its use-by or expiration date. • Cook raw meat to minimum internal temperatures. • Prevent cross-contamination between raw or undercooked food and ready-to-eat food. • Avoid using unpasteurized dairy products. • Control time and temperature.

Seafood Dated 90days

Bacteria	Shiga toxin-producing *Escherichia coli (ess-chur-EE-kee-UH KO-LI)*(STEC), also known as *E. coli.* It includes O157:H7, O26:H7, O26:H11, O111:H8, and O158:NM
Illness	Hemorrhagic colitis *(hem-or-RA-jik ko-LI-tiss)*

Shiga toxin-producing *E. coli* can be found in the intestines of cattle. It is also found in infected people. The bacteria can contaminate meat during slaughtering. Eating only a small amount of the bacteria can make a person sick. Once eaten, it produces toxins in the intestines, which causes the illness. The bacteria are often in a person's feces for weeks after symptoms have ended.

Food Commonly Linked with the Bacteria	Most Common Symptoms	Prevention Measures
• Ground beef (raw and undercooked) • Contaminated produce	• Diarrhea (eventually becomes bloody) • Abdominal cramps • Kidney failure (in severe cases)	• Cook food, especially ground beef, to minimum internal temperatures. • Purchase produce from approved, reputable suppliers. • Prevent cross-contamination between raw meat and ready-to-eat food. • Keep staff with diarrhea out of the operation. • Keep staff who have diarrhea and have been diagnosed with hemorrhagic colitis out of the operation. • Control time and temperature.

Bacteria	*Clostridium perfringens*
Illness	*Clostridium perfringens* gastroenteritis *(klos-TRID-ee-um per-FRIN-jins GAS-tro-EN-ter-I-tiss)*

Clostridium perfringens is found in dirt, where it forms spores that allow it to survive. It is also carried in the intestines of both animals and humans.

Clostridium perfringens does not grow at refrigeration temperatures. It does grow rapidly in food in the temperature danger zone. Commercially prepped food is not often involved in outbreaks. People who get sick usually do not have nausea, fever, or vomiting.

Food Commonly Linked with the Bacteria	Most Common Symptoms	Prevention Measures
• Meat • Poultry • Dishes made with meat and poultry, such as stews and gravies	• Diarrhea • Severe abdominal pain	• Cool and reheat food correctly. • Hold food at the correct temperatures. • Control time and temperature.

Bacteria   *Clostridium botulinum (klos-TRID-ee-um BOT-chew-LINE-um)*
Illness   *Botulism (BOT-chew-liz-um)*

Clostridium botulinum forms spores that are often found in water and dirt. These spores can contaminate almost any food. The bacteria do not grow well in refrigerated or highly acidic food or in food with low moisture. However, *Clostridium botulinum* grows without oxygen and can produce a lethal toxin when food is time-temperature abused. Without medical treatment, death is likely.

Food Commonly Linked with the Bacteria	Most Common Symptoms	Prevention Measures
• Incorrectly canned food	Initially	• Hold, cool, and reheat food correctly.
• Reduced-oxygen packaged (ROP) food	• Nausea and vomiting	• Inspect canned food for damage.
• Temperature-abused vegetables, such as baked potatoes	Later	• Control time and temperature.
• Untreated garlic-and-oil mixtures	• Weakness	
	• Double vision	
	• Difficulty in speaking and swallowing	

Bacteria   *Campylobacter jejuni (Camp-ee-lo-BAK-ter jay-JUNE-ee)*
Illness   *Campylobacteriosis (CAMP-ee-lo-BAK-teer-ee-O-sis)*

Though *Campylobacter jejuni* is commonly associated with poultry, it has been known to contaminate water. Illness often occurs when poultry is incorrectly cooked and when raw poultry has been allowed to cross-contaminate other food and food-contact surfaces. Campylobacteriosis is best controlled through correct cooking and the prevention of cross-contamination.

Food Commonly Linked with the Bacteria	Most Common Symptoms	Prevention Measures
• Poultry	• Diarrhea (may be watery or bloody)	• Cook food, particularly poultry, to required minimum internal temperatures.
• Water contaminated with the bacteria	• Abdominal cramps	• Prevent cross-contamination between raw poultry and ready-to-eat food.
• Meats	• Fever	• Control time and temperature.
• Stews/gravies	• Vomiting	
	• Headaches	

Bacteria   Nontyphoidal *Salmonella (SAL-me-NEL-uh)*
Illness   Salmonellosis *(SAL-men-uh-LO-sis)*

Many farm animals carry nontyphoidal *Salmonella* naturally. Eating only a small amount of these bacteria can make a person sick. How severe symptoms are depends on the health of the person and the amount of bacteria eaten. The bacteria are often in a person's feces for weeks after symptoms have ended.

Food Commonly Linked with the Bacteria

- Poultry and eggs
- Meat
- Milk and dairy products
- Produce, such as tomatoes, peppers, and cantaloupes

Most Common Symptoms

- Diarrhea
- Abdominal cramps

Vomiting

- Fever

Prevention Measures

- Cook poultry and eggs to minimum internal temperatures.
- Prevent cross-contamination between poultry and ready-to-eat food.
- Keep food handlers who are vomiting or have diarrhea and have been diagnosed with an illness from nontyphoidal Salmonella out of the operation.

Bacteria   *Salmonella* Typhi *(SAL-me-NEL-uh Ti-fee)*
Illness   Typhoid fever

Salmonella Typhi lives only in humans. People with typhoid fever carry the bacteria in their bloodstream and intestinal tract. Eating only a small amount of these bacteria can make a person sick. The severity of symptoms depends on the health of the person and the amount of bacteria eaten. The bacteria are often in a person's feces for weeks after symptoms have ended.

Food Commonly Linked with the Bacteria

- Ready-to-eat food
- Beverages

Most Common Symptoms

- High fever
- Weakness
- Abdominal pain
- Headache
- Loss of appetite
- Rash

Prevention Measures

- Exclude food handlers who have been diagnosed with an illness caused by *Salmonella* Typhi from the operation.
- Wash hands.
- Cook food to minimum internal temperatures.
- Prevent cross-contamination.

Bacteria   *Shigella* spp. *(shi-GEL-uh)*
Illness   *Shigellosis (SHIG-uh-LO-sis)*

Shigella spp. is found in the feces of humans with the illness. Most illnesses occur when people eat or drink contaminated food or water. Flies can also transfer the bacteria from feces to food. Eating only a small amount of these bacteria can make a person sick. High levels of the bacteria are often in a person's feces for weeks after symptoms have ended.

Food Commonly Linked with the Bacteria	Most Common Symptoms	Prevention Measures
• Food that is easily contaminated by hands, such as salads containing TCS food (potato, tuna, shrimp, macaroni, and chicken) • Food that has made contact with contaminated water, such as produce	• Bloody diarrhea • Abdominal pain and cramps • Fever (occasionally)	• Exclude food handlers who have diarrhea and have been diagnosed with an illness caused by *Shigella* spp. from the operation. • Wash hands. • Control flies inside and outside the operation. • Practice personal hygiene.

Bacteria   *Staphylococcus aureus (STAF-uh-lo-KOK-us OR-ee-us)*
Illness   *Staphylococcal gastroenteritis (STAF-ul-lo-KOK-al GAS-tro-EN-ter-I-tiss)*

Staphylococcus aureus can be found in humans—particularly in the hair, nose, and throat; and in infected cuts. It is often transferred to food when people carrying it touch these areas on their bodies and then handle food without washing their hands. If allowed to grow to large numbers in food, the bacteria can produce toxins that cause the illness when eaten. Cooking cannot destroy these toxins, so preventing bacterial growth is critical.

Food Commonly Linked with the Bacteria	Most Common Symptoms	Prevention Measures
• Food that requires handling during prepping • Salads containing TCS food (egg, tuna, chicken, and macaroni) • Deli meat	• Nausea • Vomiting and retching • Abdominal cramps	• Wash hands, particularly after touching the hair, face, or body. • Cover wounds on hands and arms. • Hold, cool, and reheat food correctly. • Practice personal hygiene.

Bacteria   *Vibrio vulnificus* and *Vibrio parahaemolyticus (VIB-ree-o vul-NIF-ih-kus and VIB-ree-o PAIR-uh-HEE-mo-lit-ih-kus)*

Illnesses   *Vibrio gastroenteritis (VIB-ree-o GAS-tro-EN-ter-I-tiss)*
              Vibrio vulnificus primary septicemia (VIB-ree-o vul-NIF-ih-kus SEP-ti-SEE-mee-uh)

These bacteria are found in the waters where shellfish are harvested. They can grow very rapidly at temperatures in the middle of the temperature danger zone. People with chronic conditions (such as diabetes or cirrhosis) who become sick from these bacteria may get primary septicemia. This severe illness can lead to death.

Food Commonly Linked with the Bacteria	Most Common Symptoms	Prevention Measures
• Oysters from contaminated water	• Diarrhea • Abdominal cramps and nausea • Vomiting • Low-grade fever and chills	• Cook oysters to minimum internal temperatures. • Purchase from approved, reputable suppliers.

Viruses

Virus   Hepatitis A *(HEP-a-TI-tiss)*

Illness   Hepatitis A

Hepatitis A is mainly found in the feces of people infected with it. The virus can contaminate water and many types of food. It is commonly linked with ready-to-eat food. However, it has also been linked with shellfish from contaminated water.

The virus is often transferred to food when infected food handlers touch food or equipment with fingers that have feces on them. Eating only a small amount of the virus can make a person sick. An infected person may not show symptoms for weeks but can be very infectious. Cooking does not destroy hepatitis A.

Food Commonly Linked with the Virus

- Ready-to-eat food
- Shellfish from contaminated water

Most Common Symptoms

- Fever (mild)
- General weakness
- Nausea
- Abdominal pain
- Jaundice (appears later)

Prevention Measures

- Exclude food handlers who have been diagnosed with hepatitis A from the operation.
- Exclude food handlers who have had jaundice for seven days or less from the operation.
- Wash hands.
- Avoid bare-hand contact with ready-to-eat food.
- Purchase shellfish from approved, reputable suppliers.
- Practice personal hygiene.

Virus   Norovirus *(NOR-o-VI-rus)*

Illness   Norovirus gastroenteritis

Like hepatitis A, Norovirus is commonly linked with ready-to-eat food. It has also been linked with contaminated water. Norovirus is often transferred to food when infected food handlers touch food or equipment with fingers that have feces on them.

Eating only a small amount of Norovirus can make a person sick. It is also very contagious. People become contagious within a few hours after eating it. The virus is often in a person's feces for days after symptoms have ended.

Food Commonly Linked with the Virus

- Ready-to-eat food
- Shellfish from contaminated water

Most Common Symptoms

- Vomiting
- Diarrhea
- Nausea
- Abdominal cramps

Prevention Measures

- Exclude food handlers who are vomiting or have diarrhea and have been diagnosed with Norovirus from the operation.
- Wash hands.
- Avoid bare-hand contact with ready-to-eat food.
- Purchase shellfish from approved, reputable suppliers.
- Practice personal hygiene.

Parasites

Parasite   *Anisakis simplex (ANN-ih-SAHK-iss SIM-plex)*
Illness   *Anisakiasis (ANN-ih-SAH-KYE-ah-sis)*

People can get sick when they eat raw or undercooked fish containing this parasite.

Food Commonly Linked with the Parasite	Most Common Symptoms	Prevention Measures
Raw and undercooked fish • Herring • Cod • Halibut • Mackerel • Pacific salmon	• Tingling in throat • Coughing up worms	• Cook fish to minimum internal temperatures. • If serving raw or undercooked fish, purchase sushi-grade fish that has been frozen to the correct time-temperature requirements. • Purchase from approved, reputable suppliers.

Parasite   *Cryptosporidium parvum (KRIP-TOH-spor-ID-ee-um PAR-vum)*
Illness   *Cryptosporidiosis (KRIP-TOH-spor-id-ee-O-sis)*

Cryptosporidium parvum can be found in the feces of infected people. Food handlers can transfer it to food when they touch food with fingers that have feces on them. Day-care and medical communities have been frequent locations of person-to-person spread of this parasite. Symptoms will be more severe in people with weakened immune systems.

Food Commonly Linked with the Parasite	Most Common Symptoms	Prevention Measures
• Contaminated water • Produce	• Watery diarrhea • Abdominal cramps • Nausea • Weight loss	• Use correctly treated water. • Keep food handlers with diarrhea out of the operation. • Wash hands. • Purchase from approved, reputable suppliers.

Parasite   *Giardia duodenalis (jee-ARE-dee-uh do-WAH-den-AL-is)*, also known as *G. lamblia* or *G. intestinalis*
Illness   *Giardiasis (JEE-are-DYE-uh-sis)*

Giardia duodenalis can be found in the feces of infected people. Food handlers can transfer the parasite to food when they touch food with fingers that have feces on them.

Food Commonly Linked with the Parasite	Most Common Symptoms	Prevention Measures
• Incorrectly treated water • Produce	Initially • Fever Later • Diarrhea • Abdominal cramps • Nausea	• Use correctly treated water. • Keep food handlers with diarrhea out of the operation. • Wash hands. • Purchase from approved, reputable suppliers.

Parasite   *Cyclospora cayetanensis (SI-klo-spor-uh KI-uh-te-NEN-sis)*

Illness   *Cyclosporiasis (SI-klo-spor-I-uh-sis)*

Cyclospora cayetanensis is a parasite that has been found in contaminated water and has been associated with produce irrigated or washed with contaminated water. It can also be found in the feces of infected people. Food handlers can transfer the parasite to food when they touch it with fingers containing feces. For this reason, food handlers with diarrhea must be excluded from the operation. It is also critical to purchase produce from approved, reputable suppliers.

Food Commonly Linked with the Parasite	Most Common Symptoms	Prevention Measures
• Incorrectly treated water • Produce such as berries, lettuce, or basil	• Nausea • Abdominal cramps • Mild fever • Diarrhea alternating with constipation • Loss of weight • Loss of appetite	• Purchase produce from approved, reputable suppliers. • Keep food handlers with diarrhea out of the operation. • Wash hands.

Toxins

Toxin   Histamine *(HISS-ta-meen)*

Illness   Scombroid poisoning *(SKOM-broyd)*

Histamine poisoning can occur when high levels of histamine in scombroid and other species of fish are eaten. When the fish are time-temperature abused, bacteria on the fish make the toxin. It cannot be destroyed by freezing, cooking, smoking, or curing.

Food Commonly Linked with the Toxin	Most Common Symptoms	Prevention Measures
• Tuna • Bonito • Mackerel • Mahimahi	Initially • Reddening of the face and neck • Sweating • Headache • Burning or tingling sensation in the mouth or throat Possibly later • Diarrhea • Vomiting	• Prevent time-temperature abuse during storage and prepping. • Purchase from approved, reputable suppliers.